NEW DIRECTIONS FOR ADULT AND CONTINUING EDUCATION

Susan Imel, *Ohio State University*
Ralph G. Brockett, *University of Tennessee, Knoxville*
EDITORS-IN-CHIEF

Using Learning to Meet the Challenges of Older Adulthood

James C. Fisher
University of Wisconsin–Milwaukee

Mary Alice Wolf
Saint Joseph College, Connecticut

EDITORS

Number 77, Spring 1998

JOSSEY-BASS PUBLISHERS
San Francisco

USING LEARNING TO MEET THE CHALLENGES OF OLDER ADULTHOOD
James C. Fisher, Mary Alice Wolf (eds.)
New Directions for Adult and Continuing Education, no. 77
Susan Imel, Ralph G. Brockett, Editors-in-Chief

Microfilm copies of issues and articles are available in 16mm and 35mm, as well as microfiche in 105mm, through University Microfilms Inc., 300 North Zeeb Road, Ann Arbor, Michigan 48106-1346.

ISSN 1052-2891   ISBN 0-7879-1164-X

NEW DIRECTIONS FOR ADULT AND CONTINUING EDUCATION is part of The Jossey-Bass Higher and Adult Education Series and is published quarterly by Jossey-Bass Inc., Publishers, 350 Sansome Street, San Francisco, California 94104-1342. Periodicals postage paid at San Francisco, California, and at additional mailing offices. Postmaster: Send address changes to New Directions for Adult and Continuing Education, Jossey-Bass Inc., Publishers, 350 Sansome Street, San Francisco, California 94104-1342.

SUBSCRIPTIONS cost $54.00 for individuals and $90.00 for institutions, agencies, and libraries.

EDITORIAL CORRESPONDENCE should be sent to the Editor-in-Chief, Susan Imel, ERIC/ACVE, 1900 Kenny Road, Columbus, Ohio 43210-1090. E-mail: imel.1@osu.edu.

Cover photograph by Wernher Krutein/PHOTOVAULT © 1990.

Jossey-Bass Web address: www.josseybass.com

Printed in the United States of America on acid-free recycled paper containing 100 percent recovered waste paper, of which at least 20 percent is postconsumer waste.

CONTENTS

Editors' Notes

A hundred years from now adult educators will marvel at the naïveté of educational gerontologists who were only beginning to understand older learners. "Why," they will exclaim, "there were actually age-specific programs!" "And those folks before 2000 were just discovering that aging is a rich developmental mine." "And they were only then learning that there are unique cognitive features of older people!" "Imagine!" It may be like telling persons from the Middle Ages that children are not just little adults or telling persons from the early 1900s that the teenage years are a particular developmental stage.

Such a retrospective suggests that we are at a turning point in our understanding of older persons and, with the ongoing research and interest of adult educators and others, we are beginning to develop a framework for connecting educational and gerontological theory. This sourcebook is intended for educators who are concerned with a growing demographic phenomenon—Americans are aging. It traces the history of the field; explores theoretical and research underpinnings; examines designs of curricula, including computer-assisted learning; and speculates on the educational needs of future populations of older adults.

For an understanding of the current status of older adults, knowledge of basic demographics is necessary. It is a fact of American life that we are an aging society. We have always had elders in the culture, but we now see a burgeoning of this population. In 1900, life expectancy was 49 years; today it is 75.5 years (72 for men and 78.9 for women) (Administration on Aging, 1997; U.S. Bureau of the Census, 1996). In 1900, 3 percent of the population (31 million persons) of the United States was over the age of 65; in 1998 the figure is 13 percent and represents over 32 million Americans (American Association of Retired Persons, 1996)! In the year 2030, this group will comprise 21.1 percent of the total population, approximately 66 million Americans (Administration on Aging, 1997; Baker, 1994; U.S. Bureau of the Census, 1996).

The concept of a growing population of older persons challenges the nation as a whole. The change in economic structure that will accompany this demographic reality mandates a significant role for education: teaching new skills for coping with age-related phenomena such as leisure, retirement, housing, health, death, finances, families, and political realities. For example, increased knowledge of activities leading to wellness throughout the lifespan will reduce the demand on health resources and illuminate the role that education will play in this critical area (American Association of Retired Persons, 1994; Friedman, 1993; U.S. Department of Education, National Center for Education Statistics, 1996; National Institutes of Health, and National Institute on Aging, 1993).

This sourcebook views learning as a response to the various challenges confronting older adults and describes that learning within the context of present practice and future challenges. At the same time, it explores the structural underpinnings of learning patterns of older adults. Combining theory and research in educational gerontology with the practice of older adult learning and education, it explores issues and policies related to older adult education in academic and community settings.

The first chapter describes the development of the field of educational gerontology and lays the foundation for further discussion. Roger Hiemstra describes the relationship between educational gerontology and adult education and summarizes the groundwork of Howard McClusky. In Chapter Two, Mary Alice Wolf explores theoretical underpinnings of gerontology and discusses the emerging needs of older adults relative to current and future demographic shifts.

In Chapter Three, James C. Fisher examines current research streams in educational gerontology, summarizing their findings and impact on practice. Suggesting a research agenda, Fisher notes important issues and areas of practice. In Chapter Four, Mary-Jane Eisen overviews current practice and innovative programs in older adult learning. Chapter Five reviews related policy impacts including the need for program evaluation and establishment of qualifications and credentials for teachers. David A. Peterson and Hiromi Masunaga also point out that leadership is needed in the development of policy in the field. In Chapter Six, Sandra Timmermann focuses on the role of technology in older adult learning, examining its present and future impact on educational programs for older adults.

Chapter Seven turns us to the future of the field, focusing on the next cohorts. C. Joanne Grabinski discusses the impact of succeeding cohorts, such as baby boomers and generation Xers, on the role and practice of older adult learning. In the Epilogue, James C. Fisher and Mary Alice Wolf identify important issues raised by the themes introduced in the sourcebook and explore future directions for study, practice, and research.

We believe that this overview of current research and practice will lay the groundwork for practitioners to explore further the fascinating area of older adult learning and to develop their own responses to the challenges ahead as we participate in the continuing development of the field of educational gerontology.

Mary Alice Wolf
James C. Fisher

References

Administration on Aging. *Aging into the 21st Century*. Bethesda, Md.: National Aging Information Center, May 31, 1997.

American Association of Retired Persons. *Profile of Older Americans*. Washington, D.C.: American Association of Retired Persons, 1996.

American Association of Retired Persons. *Directory of Learning Opportunities for Older Persons.* Washington, D.C.: American Association of Retired Persons, 1994.

Baker, A. J. "Baby Boomers: Education in Retirement." *The Older Learner,* 1994, 2 (1), 1–4.

Friedman, E. "Health Care's Changing Face: The Demographics of the 21st Century." *Hospitals,* 1993, 65 (7), 36–40.

National Institutes of Health, and National Institute on Aging. *Special Report on Aging 1993: Older Americans Can Expect to Live Longer and Healthier Lives.* Washington, D.C.: U.S. Department of Health and Human Services, 1993 (NIH 93–3409).

United States Bureau of the Census. *65+ in the United States.* Washington, D.C.: U.S. Government Printing Office, 1996.

United States Department of Education, National Center for Education Staticstics. "The Condition of Education 1996, Indicator 14." [http://www.ed.gov/NCES/pubs/ce/c9614a01.html].

MARY ALICE WOLF is professor of human development and gerontology and director of the Institute in Gerontology at Saint Joseph College, West Hartford, Connecticut.

JAMES C. FISHER is associate professor of adult and continuing education at the University of Wisconsin–Milwaukee.

Educational gerontology as a recognizable field has been in existence for at least twenty-five years. This chapter focuses on the history of the field from the early work of Howard McClusky through the developing body of literature and research.

From Whence Have We Come? The First Twenty-Five Years of Educational Gerontology

Roger Hiemstra

Throughout the history of humankind, adults have had to learn all their lives just to survive. In terms of recorded history, adult education efforts have received recognition of various kinds. Grattan (1955) notes that ancient Greek and Roman empires, for example, had schools, books, libraries, public recitals, theater, forums, and debates among their educational opportunities. Medieval education for adults existed, but it often was religious in nature. The British Empire developed schools for adults as early as 1811 (Grattan, 1955).

In the United States, since European domination began, the education of adults has been noted and described. In fact, the belief in creating an informed citizenry through education or religious education efforts was a hallmark of this early history, as were apprenticeship training and evening schools. Lending libraries for use by people of all ages existed as early as 1696 (Stubblefield and Keane, 1994). Benjamin Franklin's development of the Junto in 1727, a study and discussion group, was a natural extension of these educational efforts (Grattan, 1955). The Junto led to the development of a subscription library and other learning organizations. The Lyceum lecture series in the early 1800s and the Chautauqua movement that provided religious education and other study forms throughout much of the country in the late 1800s were some of the later innovations often noted as important predecessors of current adult education (Stubblefield and Keane, 1994).

Adult education during the twentieth century has been varied and known under various rubrics, such as Americanization efforts, literacy programs, vocational training, rural education, cooperative extension, university extension,

NEW DIRECTIONS FOR ADULT AND CONTINUING EDUCATION, no. 77, Spring 1998 © Jossey-Bass Publishers

community education, military education, religious education, and training or human resource development. However, educational programming aimed at or used specifically by older adults early in this century was quite limited or at least not recorded separately by educators.

Adult Education in Relationship to Educational Gerontology

Specific educational programming for older learners began after 1950 primarily as an extension of existing adult education efforts. Peterson (1983, p. 25) notes that one of the earliest comprehensive surveys of older learners was Donahue's 1955 survey: "[The survey] . . . indicated that a wide variety of instructional programs were underway by the mid 1950s but that many of these began by simply including older people in the organization's or agency's existing educational programs." But even then Donahue found older learners participating in programs sponsored by a wide variety of organizations, including "public schools, colleges, university extension, agricultural extension, correspondence [schools], libraries, state agencies, federal agencies, employment agencies, institutions, business and industry, government, and unions" (Peterson, 1983, p. 25).

Since this early survey, most studies have reported a growing number of older adults involved in learning. In research I conducted two decades ago, adults (average age nearly 70) were engaged in learning three hundred or more hours a year (Hiemstra, 1975, 1976). Adair and Mowsesian (1993), Brockett (1982), Estrin (1985), Fisher (1986), Galbraith and James (1984) are only a few of the researchers reporting similar findings.

Many programs designed specifically to meet older learner needs have developed in the past twenty to thirty years (Wenzel-Miller, 1996). Elderhostel may be the most famous; Thorson and Waskel (1990, p. 346) note that "largely self-financed and in many cases almost entirely separate from [any] . . . institutional sponsorship . . ., Elderhostel has grown to involve thousands of bright and vigorous older adults in hundreds of creative, innovative learning programs." Founded in 1974 (Knowlton, 1977), today more than two hundred thousand older adults participate annually in various Elderhostel programs both in the United States and other countries.

Another popular program for older learners is the University of Kentucky Donovan Scholars. Adults 65 and older may participate in graduate or undergraduate courses tuition free. Other Donovan features include noncredit courses, a forum series, a discussion series, and an annual writing workshop (James, 1991; Kidd, 1989). Various other learning opportunities around the country are available (Clough, 1992; Durr, Fortin, and Leptak, 1992; Hiemstra, 1994; Houston, 1991; Maxwell, 1991).

No doubt even greater numbers will participate in future programs ranging from college courses to workplace initiatives. For example, Wright (1997) optimistically reports that even the job picture has brightened for older workers up to age 70 as more companies realize the value of having mature work-ers—workers whose experiences and abilities to respond to targeted training pay off immediately through their positive values and work ethic.

Long (1990, p. 325) also suggests the future presents some challenges: "Mighty forces are exerting powerful influences on the loosely organized and vaguely defined area known as educational gerontology. . . . [They] include the demographic phenomenon referred to as the aging of the Baby Boomers, ris-ing educational achievement levels, social trends and life-styles, economic trends, and electronic advances." Each of these trends or changes will repre-sent natural maturation problems as educational gerontology moves into its second twenty-five years. Like the adult education field before it, such prob-lems become exciting challenges to face and conquer.

Howard Yale McClusky's Contribution to Educational Gerontology

Selecting one person as the founding father of a new field has its own chal-lenge because so many have made important contributions. For example, Wilma Donahue made tremendous contributions. Her 1955 book, *Education for Later Maturity,* was the first major work to identify educational needs of the aging person. David Peterson's work in defining the term "educational geron-tology" (1976), identifying graduate training efforts throughout the country (1986), and work with the Leonard Davis School of Gerontology at the Uni-versity of Southern California exemplify an outstanding professional commit-ment. Barry Lumsden's long editorship of *Educational Gerontology* and other important scholarship efforts (Sherron and Lumsden, 1990) truly have helped shape the field. So many others could be described here, but space does not permit their acknowledgment.

However, in my view no single person better exemplifies the development of educational gerontology, especially its relationship to adult education, than Howard Yale McClusky. His pioneering involvement with the education of adults and natural evolution into work with the aging person have served to guide the efforts of many people striving to meet educational gerontology's challenges.

Born in 1900 in New York, McClusky spent most of his adult life at the University of Michigan until his death in 1981. He began his career at the Uni-versity in 1924 as an instructor and received a doctorate in psychology from the University of Chicago in 1929. He rose steadily through the academic ranks, becoming a full professor in 1939. He served as a central administrator in the late thirties, but his passion and professional dedication always remained with the academic side. During his academic career, he published hundreds of jour-nal articles, monographs, book chapters, books, and other scholarly material.

McClusky's professional interests initially lay with youth as he worked in various ways with the University of Michigan School of Education to prepare teachers and to work directly with youth themselves. However, these interests changed somewhat in step with his own aging process. By the late forties, he was working with the burgeoning adult education field and established and chaired the University of Michigan's graduate department of community adult education in 1948. He became the first president of the newly formed Adult Education Association of the United States of America in 1951. He received the prestigious Delbert Clark Adult Education Award in 1956 and was a founding member of the Commission of Professors of Adult Education in 1957. In 1964 he was appointed Senior Consultant in Adult Education by the United States Office of Education and became instrumental in several corresponding federal initiatives that funded or improved adult education efforts around the country.

As he entered his middle years, McClusky's interests in the older adult started to emerge. Perhaps his first contribution to what would become educational gerontology was a paper entitled "Adult Education and Aging," presented as part of a panel at the 1950 American Educational Research Association meeting in Atlantic City. He also participated in the 1961 White House Conference on Aging and reviewed various recommendations developed there.

One of McClusky's most well-known contributions to educational gerontology was his educational background paper for the 1971 White House Conference on Aging (McClusky, 1971). He also co-chaired that conference's Section on Aging and helped develop the subsequent proceedings. The background paper and proceedings became a cornerstone for much of the thinking and scholarship since then regarding the aging person's educational potential. McClusky's own words (1973, p. 2) set the scene for much of this subsequent research and writing: "When we turn to education we find a more optimistic domain. In fact, education is itself essentially an affirmative enterprise. For instance, education for older persons is based on the assumption that it will lead to something better in the lives of those participating. It also proceeds on the collateral assumption that older persons are capable of a constructive response to educational stimulation."

Peterson (1983, p. 27) talks about the importance of McClusky's work with the 1971 White House Conference: "Howard McClusky accurately reflected . . . [a] new orientation of the 1970s when he changed the emphasis by pointing out the positive nature of education and the potential that every person, regardless of age, has. His statements that education was an affirmative enterprise that resulted in positive outcomes have been quoted on numerous occasions and have proved to be the orientation of the field. . . ."

McClusky discusses his natural evolution into work with the older adult: "I have come into the field of gerontology from the domain of adult education. The gerontological movement is geared pretty much to the protection of older people and the production of a floor of support, so that older people can live in dignity and self-respect and as independently as possible. This is as it should be. But the educational approach is a little different. As educators, we assume that the client is capable of improvement" (1976, p. 118).

Thus, because of its faith in the learning ability of older persons and because of its confidence in the improvement that results from learning, education in contrast with other areas in the field of aging can be invested with a climate of optimism that is highly attractive to those who may be involved in its operation (McClusky, 1973, p. 2).

This positive appeal to educators of adults to realize that older adults are always capable of more, are able to learn, change, and improve throughout life, has resulted in much research, understanding, and improved ways of working with the older adult learner. McClusky put it this way (1976, p. 119): "So what I am saying is that if we approach the field of gerontology from an educational standpoint, we constantly see evidence of the fact that older people are learning and can renew their faith in their ability to learn. As a consequence, we must find ways to help people rediscover, reinvigorate, and reactivate their latent interests and talents they never thought they had."

Dr. McClusky also contributed some original thinking that has impacted on the educational gerontology field in various ways. He is perhaps best known for his theory of margin (1970, p. 27): "*Margin* is a function of the relationship of load to power. By *load* we mean the self and social demands required by a person to maintain a minimal level of autonomy. By *power* we mean the resources, i.e., abilities, possessions, position, allies, etc., which a person can command in coping with load."

This theory is best visualized as a formula (McClusky, 1963):

$$\text{Margin} = \frac{\text{load}}{\text{power}}$$

Surplus power, the denominator, represents a margin or cushion for handling various load components, such as external living tasks or internal or personal life expectancies. McClusky notes that his load-power ratio is useful "in describing the amount of margin involved in adult adjustment" (1963, p. 41). The goal is to help the older person learn how to maintain a surplus of power: "For example, if the aging person could replace the load required by the achievement of upward mobility or by the maintenance of social status with the load or tasks of community services, or the preservation of things (natural or manmade) of beauty, and if by a program of study and training the older person could increase his ability to engage in such activities, his resulting margin could conceivably be more productive, satisfying, and growth-inducing than anything done earlier in life. . . . [Thus] education can be, if properly conceived and implemented, a major force in the achievement of this outcome" (McClusky, n.d., p. 330).

Numerous implications exist for educators of older learners from McClusky's conceptual work with the theory of margin (Hiemstra, 1993; James, 1986). Main (1979), for example, developed some teaching strategies based on power and load notions. I developed several ideas for measuring, evaluating, and planning appropriate educational experiences based on load and power imbalances (Hiemstra, 1981).

McClusky's categories of need (1971) emerged from his work with margin theory. He created five distinct need categories as means for developing programs for older learners:

1. Coping needs—minimal literacy and self-sufficiency levels; if these needs are not met a surplus of power to meet higher needs is absent. Coping needs "must be satisfied in order for adequate social adjustment, psychological health, and physical well-being to continue" (Sherron and Lumsden, 1990, p. 281).
2. Expressive needs—activity carried out for its own sake; time is usually required by each person for some expressive activity, such as "the needs for involvement in activities for the sake of the pleasure the activity gives" (p. 281).
3. Contributive needs—altruistic desire to serve others; surplus margin is utilized outside of "self" or coping requirements. "McClusky believes older people represent a reservoir of wisdom and experience that society needs but has not yet learned to exploit" (p. 282).
4. Influence needs—desire for political skill and wisdom; surplus energy and resources may go to improving related skills. "[T]his kind of need is actually the need to affect the direction and quality of life" (p. 282).
5. Transcendence needs—rising above age-related limitations; learning to balance power and load. "This kind of need may well be satisfied as a by-product of the gratification of another need" (p. 282).

This five-part framework has been utilized by various people in program design efforts. Graney and Hays (1976), for example, suggest that the framework provides a useful hierarchy for guiding appropriate educational practice.

McClusky (1990, p. 60) also promoted an interaction between generations in terms of educational programming and what he called the community of generations: "The concept of the *community of generations* is an intentional variation on a life-span approach to comprehending the wholeness of life. It is based on the assumption that, although separated by time and experience, each generation nevertheless has a common stake with other generations in relating itself to the wholeness of the life-span of which it is a part."

Throughout his professional life, McClusky demonstrated a belief that each person has tremendous potential for change, growth, and development. He urged all of us to find ways of maximizing this potential such that the later years are enhanced by personal ability (1976, p. 11): "The task of society is to produce a generation of persons in the later years who are models of lifelong fulfillment for the emulation and guidance of oncoming generations and that life at its best in the later years should be a guide for education at all earlier years of life leading thereto."

The Evolving Discipline of Educational Gerontology

Educational gerontology as a recognizable field has existed for at least twenty-five years. "Probably the first institutional use of the term educational gerontology was at the University of Michigan, where a graduate program of that name was established in 1970 within the School of Education" (Peterson, 1976, p. 61). It is fitting that Howard McClusky, although officially retired in 1968, served as chair of the program from 1973 to 1974.

Peterson (1976, p. 62) defines educational gerontology as "the study and practice of instructional endeavors for and about aged and aging individuals. It can be viewed as having three distinct, although interrelated, aspects: (1) educational endeavors designed for persons who are middle aged and older; (2) educational endeavors for a general or specific public about aging and older people; and (3) educational preparation of persons who are working or intend to be employed in serving older people in professional or paraprofessional capacities."

Bramwell (1985) looked at several criteria to assess whether gerontology is a separate discipline. He feels it does not match these criteria, yet it is being taught as a separate discipline in many universities. Peterson (1986) notes that the number of campuses offering at least one course related to educational gerontology has nearly doubled in the previous nine years. Obviously ongoing research is required to determine whether or not educational gerontology can be treated as a separate discipline.

Summary

As a backdrop for subsequent chapters in this sourcebook, I examined how the field has been defined through its research during the past two decades. I carried out an informal content analysis of articles published in *Educational Gerontology* since its inception in 1976 and let the categories emerge as I examined their contents.

As Table 1.1 shows, I chose fairly broad descriptors. I sometimes combined topics I deemed similar in nature. Occasionally, I placed an article into two categories when an equal representation seemed apparent. I also decided not to categorize any article written by authors from outside of the United States or Canada or any article that was written about some international program or issues. Many of the sixty-four international articles were related to other categories but I leave to future researchers more specific analysis of their content.

Such topic diversity will not be a surprise to readers who are familiar with literature in the field. Several categories represent articles published regularly since 1976. Others, such as computers and technology, represent articles primarily written in the past few years. The miscellaneous category represents a wide range of topics or issues, with fewer than six articles per topic.

Table 1.2 portrays emerging issues, those issues likely to receive additional articles in the near future. In addition, like its parent discipline, adult education,

Table 1.1. Categories of *Educational Gerontology* Articles, 1976–1996

Category Descriptor	Number of Articles	Percent of Total[*]
Health and fitness	100	10.7
Attitudes toward aging	69	7.4
International issues	64	6.8
Higher education	63	6.7
Administrative issues	61	6.5
Training/instruction issues	55	5.9
Memory issues	52	5.6
Cognitive issues	51	5.5
Educational issues	41	4.4
Miscellaneous	37	4.0
Old age in literature	31	3.3
Reading/reading ability	25	2.7
Women's issues	25	2.7
Retirement/pre-retirement issues	22	2.4
Computers/technology	21	2.2
Life satisfaction issues	19	2.0
Communication issues	18	1.9
Counseling issues	18	1.9
Creativity/art/music/drama	18	1.9
Knowledge of aging	18	1.9
Policy issues/tuition policies	17	1.8
Needs or interests	16	1.7
Philosophy/religion/ethics	14	1.5
Intergenerational issues	13	1.4
Special elderly populations	13	1.4
Learning resources/services	12	1.3
Research issues	12	1.3
Rural issues	12	1.3
Sexuality issues	9	0.7
Social service issues	9	0.7

[*]Percentage of total number of articles represented in this table.

Table 1.2. Emerging *Educational Gerontology* Categories

Category Descriptor	Number of Articles	Percent of Total[*]
Careers related to aging	8	13.1
Community and aging issues	8	13.1
Death and dying	8	13.1
Grandparenting	7	11.5
Geriatrics	6	9.8
Literacy/illiteracy	6	9.8
Nursing homes	6	9.8
Participation	6	9.8
State of the art	6	9.8

[*]Percentage of total number of articles represented in this table.

educational gerontology as a field of study no doubt will see increasing numbers of authors looking at retrospective issues, such as the field's history, assessments of its future, and biographical work on early leaders.

The remainder of this sourcebook examines and expands on various topics identified in previous research. Such areas as new or emerging educational approaches, current research streams, current practices or policies, the emerging role of technology, and future directions are covered. Adult education has spawned an exciting and growing field of study, and this sourcebook helps further our understanding of this dynamic.

References

Adair, S. R., and Mowsesian, R. "The Meanings and Motivation of Learning During the Retirement Transition." *Educational Gerontology,* 1993, *19* (4), 317–330.

Bramwell, R. D. "Gerontology as a Discipline." *Educational Gerontology,* 1985, *11* (4–6), 201–210.

Brockett, R. G. "Self-Directed Learning Readiness and Life Satisfaction Among Older Adults." Unpublished doctoral dissertation, Adult Education Program, Syracuse University, 1982.

Clough, B. "Broadening Perspectives on Learning Activities in Later Life." *Educational Gerontology,* 1992, *18* (5), 447–459.

Donahue, W. T. (ed.). *Education for Later Maturity.* New York: Whiteside, 1955.

Durr, D., Fortin, S., and Leptak, J. "Effective Art Education for Older Adults." *Educational Gerontology,* 1992, *18* (2), 149–161.

Estrin, H. R. "Life Satisfaction and Participation in Learning Activities Among Widows." Unpublished doctoral dissertation, Adult Education Program, Syracuse University, 1985.

Fisher, J. C. "Participation in Educational Activities by Active Older Adults." *Adult Education Quarterly,* 1986, *36* (4), 202–210.

Galbraith, M. W., and James, W. B. "Assessment of Dominant Perceptual Learning Styles of Older Adults." *Educational Gerontology,* 1984, *10* (6), 449–458.

Graney, M. J., and Hays, W. C. "Senior Students: Higher Education After Age 62." *Educational Gerontology,* 1976, *1* (4), 343–360.

Grattan, C. H. *In Quest of Knowledge.* New York: Association Press, 1955.

Hiemstra, R. *The Older Adult and Learning.* Lincoln: Department of Adult and Continuing Education, University of Nebraska–Lincoln, 1975. (ED 006 003)

Hiemstra, R. "The Older Adult's Learning Projects." *Educational Gerontology,* 1976, *1* (4), 331–342.

Hiemstra, R. "The Contributions of Howard Yale McClusky to an Evolving Discipline of Educational Gerontology." *Educational Gerontology,* 1981, *6* (2–3), 209–226.

Hiemstra, R. "Three Underdeveloped Models for Adult Learning." In S. B. Merriam (ed.), *An Update on Adult Learning Theory.* New Directions for Adult and Continuing Education, no. 57. San Francisco: Jossey-Bass, 1993.

Hiemstra, R. "Lifelong Education and Personal Growth." In A. Monk (ed.), *The Columbia Retirement Handbook.* New York: Columbia University Press, 1994.

Houston, P. "A New Breed of Retirement Community." *Newsweek,* Nov. 11, 1991, p. 62.

James, J. M. "Instructor-Generated Load: An Inquiry Based on McClusky's Concepts of Margin." Unpublished doctoral dissertation, Department of Educational Administration and Adult Education, University of Wyoming, 1986.

James, R. H. (ed.). *Second Spring.* Vol. 22, No. 1. Lexington: Donovan Scholars Program, University of Kentucky, 1991.

Kidd, R., Jr. "Donovan Program Draws Seniors from Other States." In *Donovan Scholars 25th Anniversary.* Lexington: Donovan Scholars Program, University of Kentucky, 1989.

Knowlton, M. P. "Liberal Arts: The Elderhostel Plan for Survival. *Educational Gerontology,* 1977, *2* (1), 87–94.

Long, H. B. "Trends and Development in 2000–2010." *Educational Gerontology,* 1990, *16* (4), 317–326.

Main, K. "The Power-Load-Margin Formula of Howard Y. McClusky as the Basis for a Model of Teaching." *Adult Education,* 1979, *30* (1), 19–33.

Maxwell, R. B. "Education: Window to Fulfillment. *Modern Maturity,* 1991, *34* (3), 10–11.

McClusky, H. Y. "Education for Aging: The Scope of the Field and Perspectives for the Future." In S. M. Grabowski and W. D. Mason (eds.), *Learning for Aging.* Washington, D.C.: Adult Education Association of the United States of America, n.d.

McClusky, H. Y. "Course of the Adult Life Span." In W. C. Hallenbeck (ed.), *Psychology of Adults.* Chicago: Adult Education Association of the United States of America, 1963.

McClusky, H. Y. "A Dynamic Approach to Participation in Community Development." *Journal of Community Development Society,* 1970, *1* (1), 25–32.

McClusky, H. Y. *Education: Background Paper for 1971 White House Conference on Aging.* Washington, D.C.: White House Conference on Aging, 1971.

McClusky, H. Y. "Co-Chairman's Statement (Section on Education)." *Toward a National Policy on Aging.* Final report, Vol. II, White House Conference on Aging. Washington, D.C.: U.S. Government Printing Office, 1973.

McClusky, H. Y. "What Research Says About Adult Learning Potential and Teaching Older Adults." In R. M. Smith (ed.), *Adult Learning: Issues and Innovations.* DeKalb, Ill.: ERIC Clearinghouse in Career Education, Department of Secondary and Adult Education, Northern Illinois University, 1976.

McClusky, H. Y. "The Community of Generations: A Goal and a Context for the Education of Persons in the Later Years." In R. H. Sherron and D. B. Lumsden (eds.), *Introduction to Educational Gerontology.* (3rd ed.). New York: Hemisphere, 1990.

Peterson, D. A. "Educational Gerontology: The State of the Art." *Educational Gerontology,* 1976, *1* (1), 61–73.

Peterson, D. A. *Facilitating Education for Older Learners.* San Francisco: Jossey-Bass, 1983.

Peterson, D. A. "Extent of Gerontology Instruction in American Institutions of Higher Education." *Educational Gerontology,* 1986, *12* (6), 519–529.

Sherron, R. H., and Lumsden, D. B. (eds.). *Introduction to Educational Gerontology.* (3rd ed.). New York: Hemisphere, 1990.

Stubblefield, H. W., and Keane, P. *Adult Education in the American Experience: From the Colonial Period to the Present.* San Francisco: Jossey-Bass, 1994.

Thorson, J. A., and Waskel, S. A. "Educational Gerontology and the Future." In R. H. Sherron and D. B. Lumsden (eds.), *Introduction to Educational Gerontology.* (3rd ed.). New York: Hemisphere, 1990.

Wenzel-Miller, L. A. "Serving the Needs of the Older Adult Learner." *Catalyst,* 1996, *25* (2), 7–10.

Wright, J. "Job Picture of Older Workers Brightens." *The Charlotte Observer,* July 23, 1997, p. 15A.

ROGER HIEMSTRA *is visiting professor of adult education at Elmira College, Elmira, New York.*

This chapter explores the current theoretical underpinnings of educational gerontology and looks at older adults' emerging learning needs.

New Approaches to the Education of Older Adults

Mary Alice Wolf

This chapter discusses factors that serve as the foundation for program development for older learners, including developmental perspectives, longitudinal research into lifespan habits, gender roles, reminiscence, cognition, and need-based learning.

Developmental Perspectives

A number of theories can be used as a framework to explore development in older adulthood. Most useful is the theory of Erik Erikson (1963, 1981, 1982, and 1986 with Erikson and Kivnick), who explored the nature of psychosocial tasks that individuals accomplish at specific stages in life. For this discussion, the last two stages, generativity and integrity, are most important.

Generativity. Generativity can be observed in the many ways that older people contribute to the lives of younger persons. According to Erikson, mature individuals have a mandate to support the development of the next generation. Educational opportunities for this developmental task can be found in church settings, grandparenting organizations, tutoring, and other arenas. In a group of retired adults attending leadership training at a center in North Carolina, 78 percent had turned to volunteerism (Manheimer and Snodgrass, 1993). These older adults worked an average of 9.3 hours each week as public school tutors, in the Red Cross, in synagogues, in retirement communities, and in adult day-care centers. Generativity through education and "creative retirement" (Manheimer, 1992) is a vibrant concept in the lives of many older adults. In a sample of "elderlearners," ages 55 to 96, Lamdin (1997) found that 72.9 percent volunteered within their communities. Interestingly, many older adults

NEW DIRECTIONS FOR ADULT AND CONTINUING EDUCATION, no. 77, Spring 1998 © Jossey-Bass Publishers

participate in research in cognitive and health domains (Besdine, 1997; Schaie, 1989; Schaie and Willis; 1996, Vaillant, 1997). "I feel as though I'm forging new territory," said one healthy 78-year-old of her status as a research participant.

Integrity. Erikson also observed that the life cycle is epigenetic: individuals continually rework tasks of development. Older adults often seek ways to explore earlier phases of their lives through caretaking, initiating community and family projects, and renewing identity and intimacy. Kivnick recommends creating opportunities for older adults to talk about their struggles with initiative, autonomy, and intimacy, to discuss "thematic strengths that are robust and resilient" (1993, p. 15).

In the stage of *integrity,* elders often find significance in the learning they have achieved; they make meaning of their own experiences. This cannot be done in solitude; thus it is often a time of social connection. It is important for educators to recognize that learning experiences can heighten the meaning elders find in their old age. Of this time in life, Erikson theorized, "What is the last ritualization built into the style of old age? I think it is *philo-sophical:* for in maintaining some order and meaning in the dis-integration of body and mind, it can also advocate a durable hope in wisdom" (1982, p. 64). In community centers, senior centers, Elderhostels, adult learning communities, and other gathering places, older adults connect with others to affirm themselves. A recent exchange with a 78-year-old woman at a health center echoed what Erikson called "resolution and fortitude" (in Neugarten, 1996, p. 302):

RESEARCHER: "How are you?"
HILDA: "I am good. If I am here, I am good."

The need to connect, to be part of a human universe, and to grow characterizes older learners. Robert Peck observed that the ability to change is paramount to psychological well-being in older persons. He wrote, "Those people who age most 'successfully' in this stage with little psychic discomfort and with no less effectiveness are those who calmly invert their previous value hierarchy, now putting the use of their 'heads' above the use of their 'hands,' both as their standard for self-evaluation and as their chief resource for solving life problems." (1968, p. 89)

Longitudinal Underpinnings

One particularly fruitful area of developmental research has been the use of longitudinal methodologies to follow individuals through lifelong shifts. Especially important are those of Elder (1979); Erikson, Erikson, and Kivnick (1986); Holahan (1994) (who used the data from the Terman Study of the Gifted); Maas and Kuypers (1977) (who used the data from the Oakland Growth Studies); and Vaillant (1990 with Vaillant, 1993, 1995, 1997). Theory built from longitudinal studies contributes to our ability to understand individual and cohort needs that emerge within historical contexts. For example, we can follow an individual's problem-solving strategies across a long expanse rather than compare individuals in specific age groups, as cross-sectional research does. Other theoretical underpinnings include role theory approaches (Gutmann, 1964, 1975, 1987; Turner and Troll, 1994) and the social construction of aging (Gubrium, 1993; Josselson and Lieblich, 1995; Ryff and Essex, 1992). The contribution of these longitudinal underpinnings to adult learning theory and practice is profound. By understanding *how* people rely on earlier patterns of behavior, we can develop environments and modes of instruction that strengthen and capitalize on their learning styles.

Gender Roles

In cross-cultural research, Gutmann (1964, 1975, 1987) found that men and women developed in new ways after what is called the "parental imperative." In late middle age, Gutmann hypothesized, when the children are no longer in the home, gender stereotypes relax. Men, he states, no longer need to play the role of "achiever" or "aggressor." They allow their own "feminine characteristics" to emerge and can be comfortable with nurturing and interpersonal development. Women, on the other hand, can "exert some of the masculine qualities of assertion and executive capacity that they had previously had to repress" (Cooper and Gutmann, 1987, p. 347). When they are no longer responsible for children in the household, women are freer to engage in what Gutmann calls "active mastery," to develop characteristics that might have been considered "masculine." One woman described this shift (which Cooper and Gutmann refer to as the post–empty nest shift), saying, "There was some secret part of me that was locked away and then, at that time, was freed" (Cooper and Gutmann, 1987, p. 351).

Often adult male learners in cohorts over 60 engage in affiliative and nurturing roles (Wolf and Leahy, in press). A mark of this phenomenon is the growing number of older men who have started late-life careers in counseling and marriage and family therapy. When they explore aesthetics, participate in discussions of family, and engage in other activities previously considered feminine domains, they are not losing their masculinity. Women often describe themselves as having expanded "on their basic feminine gender style to include aspects that they themselves regarded as 'masculine'" (Huyck, 1994, p. 218). Yet there is a "balance that keeps them feeling securely feminine" (Huyck, 1994, p. 219). This phenomenon will change as future cohorts enter older adulthood: their gender roles have not been as tradition-bound as those of today's elders. Of this relaxation of gender stereotypes, Betty Friedan (1993a, p. 7) declared, "I just say to you, look at the strengths, look at the adventure, look at the uncharted territory, as we really take on the *full* complexity of an age that can liberate us from gender masks."

Practical and aesthetic educational experiences often support developmental mandates: for women, courses in taxation, investments, business, and travel; for men, experiences in storytelling, history, personal development, and spirituality; for both, opportunities to be generative through mentoring, counseling, and pastoral outreach. Other areas that are popular for older adults are courses in grandparenting, human development, intergenerational projects, building personal narratives, computers, the humanities, and business skills (American Association of Retired Persons (AARP), 1996; Cole, Van Tassel, and Kastenbaum, 1992; Dekker, 1993; Gibson, 1994; Greenberg, 1993; Kreitlow and Kreitlow, 1989; Lamdin, 1997; Neugarten, 1996; North Carolina Center for Creative Retirement, 1994, Shuldiner, 1992; Walker, 1996).

A highly successful quality of older adulthood is cathectic flexibility, "the capacity to shift emotional investments from one person to another and from one activity to another" (Peck, 1968, p. 89). As older adults continually rework developmental tasks and seek opportunities for healthy mastery of these tasks, they may engage parts of themselves that haven't been in use for many years (Kidder, 1993; Kivnick 1993; Vaillant, 1997; Vaillant and Vaillant, 1990.) Educational opportunities can maximize the potential of all participants, whether through direct intervention such as literacy or interpersonal skills, or through indirect support such as vocational retraining or computer mastery (Hiemstra, 1994; Hudson, 1991; Schaie and Willis, 1996). In fact, merely *deciding* to undertake a new direction is often correlated with mental and physical empowerment (Chiva, 1996; Friedan, 1993b; Langer and Rodin, 1977; Long, 1993; Solomon and others, 1992; Syme, 1990). Self-directed learning abounds in the learning tasks identified (Boggs, 1992; Brockett, 1985; Brockett and Hiemstra, 1991; Manheimer, 1992; Rodin, Schooler, and Schaie, 1990).

Reminiscence

Some gerontologists (Butler, 1963, 1982; Kaminsky, 1984; McMahon and Rhudick, 1967; Moody, 1984; Myerhoff, 1992) suggest that reminiscence and life review are pivotal to reaching integrity for older adults. Robert Butler (1963, 1982) developed the theory that active remembrance in older persons is a natural and universal process of "life review," an evaluation of one's past experiences. He wrote, "I conceive of the life review as a naturally occurring, universal mental process characterized by the progressive return to consciousness of experiences and conflicts; simultaneously, and normally, these revived experiences and conflicts can be surveyed and reintegrated" (1963, p. 66).

Although not all older adults may engage in the classic life review, an acceptance of reminiscence as normal and functional has changed the way educational gerontologists view recollection and reminiscence in late life and has charged us to organize activities that welcome older persons' telling their life stories (Wolf, 1985, 1992a, 1992b). Programmatic responses include memoir-writing workshops (Birren and Deutchman, 1991; Kaminsky, 1984, 1985; and Moody, 1984, 1988a, among others), curricula including drama and poetry (Burnside and Haight, 1994; Giltian, 1990; Lyman and Edwards, 1989; Magee, 1988a, 1988b; Merriam, 1990, Perlstein, 1988), or experiences that invite elders to connect the past with the present (Beatty and Wolf, 1996; Bornat, 1995; Gardella, 1985; Haight and Webster, 1995; Shuldiner, 1992; Wolf, 1985).

Cognitive Theory

A number of specific studies explore cognition and aging (see Fisher, Chapter Three, this volume). The majority find that older adults are fully capable of learning (Birren and Schaie, 1996). The central question is, How does learning occur and in what ways is it affected by aging? We wonder how much we can take in that is new and whether learning is different for older people. The following discussion explores some of the pivotal assertions of this body of research.

Basic to the theory of older adult learning is the concept of integrity and intellectual development culminating in wisdom (Dittmann-Kohli and Baltes, 1990; Labouvie-Vief, 1990b, Simonton, 1990). Schaie, a leader in research on cognition and aging, posits that theories of intelligence must be "multidimensional" (1990, p. 292). Measures of intelligence include spatial orientation, inductive reasoning, and fluency (Schaie and Willis, 1986, 1996). In applied educational activities, "Depending upon the age group, from 60 to 85 percent of all participants remain stable or improve on specific abilities" (Schaie, 1990, p. 296). Functioning at a stable intellectual level, then, is related to one's continued involvement in cognitive activities (Berg, 1990; Light, 1990; Schaie, 1988, 1989). Schaie writes, "It's possible that healthy individuals who maintain an active intellectual life will show little or no loss of intellectual abilities even into their eighties and beyond" (1990, p. 319).

Labouvie-Vief (1990a) proposes that intelligence and memory are adaptive and that the nature and requirements of intelligence and memory change with old age, providing opportunities to develop other adaptive skills equal to the needs of life, "a kind of intelligent pragmatism" (Labouvie-Vief, 1980, p. 7). Baltes (1993) proposes the development of "selective optimization with compensation" (p. 59) in older adults. This involves renewed "cognitive aspects of the self, self-development, and self-management" (p. 581). Indeed, many older persons have focused their learning on meeting a need for health and wellness, particularly as the Medicare system is debated and they grapple with health maintenance organizations (Besdine, 1997; Lindbloom, 1993; Moody, 1988b; Wolf, 1994). Educational interventions that are specific, pragmatic, and enhance autonomy are needed throughout the later years when frailty or ill health may occur.

Need-Based Learning

There remains no better model relating age and need than that of Abraham Maslow (1970). Individuals will seek to order their lives, to find meaning, satisfy safety and physiological needs, and achieve self-actualization in creative ways throughout the later years of life. Changing family roles, age-related losses, and social commitments impel elders to seek information. Beatty and Wolf (1996) present guidelines for connections with older adults and their families. These connections include individual, cohort, and community need-to-know patterns of personal and social transitions. This theoretical perspective promotes learning for advocacy, solving community problems, and managing finances. Much of this problem-solving education is self-directed and satisfying for older adults (Beatty and Wolf, 1996; Boggs, 1992; Brockett, 1985; Fisher, 1993; Long, 1993; Piskurich, 1993).

Self-sufficiency, the ability to remain in control of one's life, is a prime motivation for adults of all ages. Interestingly, older individuals who become deprived of this "locus of control" have been found to be especially vulnerable to illness and passive behaviors (Beatty and Wolf, 1996; Langer and Rodin, 1977; Rodin and Langer, 1977). Learning for exercise and health maintenance is essential (Deobil, 1989; Hasselkus, 1983; Peterson, Vaillant, and Seligman, 1988; Rowe and Kahn, 1987). Education for continued self-sufficiency, for community living, for vocational, retirement, health, housing, and for other concerns is ongoing (Reingold and Werby, 1990). Indeed, new ways of approaching aging, known as "successful aging" in medical gerontology and "productive aging" in political gerontology, are a part of understanding the changing role of the older adult (Rowe and Kahn, 1987). Education for autonomy for older cohorts will be essential as more "baby boomers" retire and enter the health care network (Lindbloom, 1993).

Moody (1988a, p. 191) stresses the need for education about the "information economy": "The pivotal role of the production and distribution of knowledge constitutes the economic basis for postindustrial growth." With this role, Moody predicts that older adults will become more self-reliant. He adds, "the self-help ethos includes a strong distrust of experts, skepticism about professionals, and rejection of control by outsiders. Whether in citizen activism or self-care for one's own body, self-help groups represent a demand for empowerment: for control over what is closest and most vital." (p. 171)

Conclusions

In an ongoing study by this author, a group of older learners were found to want information about "this brave new journey." They openly discussed the adjustments required by them and their cohorts. Although aging is still taboo in many quarters, many older adults were eagerly sharing creative and adaptive solutions to their new challenges. Fisher (1993) delineated age-related responses in meeting developmental challenges: these remain a benchmark for our educational model in both instrumental and expressive domains.

The needs of future cohorts of older adults will, in some ways, replicate those of today's older learners. However, we can expect different and more complex uses of the educational experience. Given increased life expectancy, mandates to learn new technologies, continuation of employment, and health care challenges, baby boomers will require extended educational opportunities as they reach age 65. This is the work of our future. Indeed, Bass, Kutza, and Torres-Gil (1990, p. xiii), in examining the challenges to policy dictated by the demographic shift, write, "*The graying of the major industrial nations* is upon us, and we have just begun to grapple with its implications. In the next century, one of every four persons in the United States—that is, nearly one in every three adults—may be 65 years old or older."

Older adults now are required to take unprecedented responsibility for their own health care decisions. Daily, we hear of elders who, having consulted two or three specialists, are left to determine the course of their treatment. In 1997, 12 percent of adults were over 65 years of age. In the year 2030, this percentage will be 24 percent. Not only are people living longer, but they are having fewer children. That means that older adults will need to expect to manage their own old age (Besdine, 1997).

Practitioners would do well to prepare themselves for the shifts that will emerge by designing programs that stimulate, challenge, and allow for development of affective and cognitive growth. We know that older adults tolerate ambiguity and tend toward age-integrated learning experiences. What a fruitful combination that might be for cross-pollination of minds, young and old! The real need exists for elders and young people to know each other: this benefits each generation. Creative environments that permit elders to be needed, to contribute to the lives of young people, would connect the two ends of the life cycle. Examples of storytelling foster grandparents, computer linkages, and workshops in the arts inspire us. Surely there is a need to reflect on the meaning of aging within the life cycle. What remains the task of adult educators is to link our future with a network of life-giving challenges to fully support the learning needs of older people and to develop greater significance for the role of learning in old age. In our present lies our future.

References

American Association of Retired Persons. *Profile of Older Americans.* Washington, D.C., 1996.

Baltes, P. B. "The Aging Mind: Potential and Limits." *The Gerontologist,* 1993, *33* (5), 580–594.

Bass, S. A., Kutza, E. A., and Torres-Gil, F. M. (eds.). *Diversity in Aging: Challenges Facing Planners & Policymakers in the 1990s.* Glenview, Ill.: Scott, Foresman, 1990.

Beatty, P. T., and Wolf, M. A. *Connecting with Older Adults: Educational Responses and Approaches.* Malabar, Fla.: Krieger, 1996.

Berg, C. A. "What Is Intellectual Efficacy Over the Life Course?: Using Adults' Conceptions to Address the Question." In J. Rodin, C. Schooler, K. W. Schaie (eds.). *Self-Directedness: Cause and Effects Throughout the Life Course.* Hillsdale, N.J.: Lawrence Erlbaum, 1990.

Besdine, R. Address at the Opening of the Claude Pepper Older Americans Independence Center. Farmington, Conn.: University of Connecticut Health Center, May 19, 1997.

Birren, J. E., and Deutchman, D. *Guiding Autobiography Groups for Older Adults.* Baltimore: The Johns Hopkins University Press, 1991.

Birren, J. E., and Schaie, K. W. (eds.). *Handbook of the Psychology of Aging.* (4th ed.) San Diego: Academic Press, 1996.

Boggs, D. L. "Learning and Action Among Older Citizens." *International Review of Education,* 1992, *38* (4), 393–402.

Brockett, R. G. "The Relationship Between Self-Directed Learning Readiness and Life Satisfaction Among Older Adults." *Adult Education Quarterly,* 1985, *35* (4), 210–219.

Brockett, R. G., and Hiemstra, R. *Self-Direction in Adult Learning: Perspectives on Theory, Research, and Practice.* New York: Routledge, 1991.

Bornat, J. (ed.). *Reminiscence Reviewed.* Philadelphia: Open University Press, 1995.

Burnside, I., and Haight, B. K. "Protocols for Reminiscence and Life Review." *Nurse Practitioner,* 1994, *19,* 55–61.

Butler, R. N. "The Interpretation of Reminiscence in the Aged." *Psychiatry,* 1963, *26,* 65–76.

Butler, R. N. "Successful Aging and the Role of the Life Review." In S. H. Zarit (ed.), *Readings in Aging and Death.* (2nd ed.) New York: Norton, 1982.

Chiva, A. "Managing Change in Mid and Later Life." In J. Walker (ed.), *Changing Concepts of Retirement.* Brookfield, Vt.: Ashgate, 1996.

Cole, T. R., Van Tassel, D. D., and Kastenbaum, R. (eds.). *Handbook of the Humanities and Aging.* New York: Springer, 1992.

Cooper, K. L., and Gutmann, D. L. "Gender Identity and Ego Mastery Style in Middle-Aged, Pre-and Post-Empty Nest Women." *The Gerontologist,* 1987, *27* (3), 347–352.

Dekker, D. "Award-Winning Older Learner Programs. *Older Adult Education News,* 1993, *1* (2), 1.

Deobil, S. "Physical Fitness for Retirees." *Health Promotion,* 1989, *4* (2), 85– 90.

Dittmann-Kohli, F., and Baltes, P. B. "Toward a Neofunctionalist Conception of Adult Intellectual Development: Wisdom as a Prototypical Case of Intellectual Growth." In C. N. Alexander and Ellen J. Langer (eds.), *Higher States of Human Development.* New York: Oxford University Press, 1990.

Elder, G. H., "Historical Change in Life Patterns and Personality." In P. B. Baltes and O. G. Brim, Jr. (eds.), *Life-Span Development and Behavior,* (Vol. 2). New York: Academic Press, 1979.

Erikson, E. H. *Childhood and Society.* New York: Norton, 1963.

Erikson, E. H. "Elements of a Psychoanalytic Theory of Psychosocial Development." In S. I. Greenspan and G. Pollock (eds.), *The Course of Life (Vol. I): Infancy and Early Childhood.* Washington, D.C.: U.S. Department of Health and Human Services, 1981.

Erikson, E. H. *The Life Cycle Completed.* (2nd ed.) New York: W. W. Norton, 1982.

Erikson, E. H., Erikson, J. M., and Kivnick, H. Q. *Vital Involvement in Old Age.* New York: Norton, 1986.

Fischer, R., Blazey, L., and Lipman, H. T. *Students of the Third Age.* New York: Macmillan, 1992.

Fisher, J. C. "A Framework for Describing Developmental Change Among Older Adults." *Adult Education Quarterly,* 1993, *43* (2), 76–89.

Friedan, B. "Breaking Through the Age Mystique." In R. Crose (ed.), *Gender and Gerontology: Women's Issues in Mental Health and Lifespan Development.* Muncie, Ind.: Ball State University, 1993a.

Friedan, B. *The Fountain of Age.* New York: Simon & Schuster, 1993b.

Gardella, L. G. "The Neighborhood Group: A Reminiscence Group for the Disoriented Old." *Social-Work-with-Groups,* 1985, *8* (2), 43–52.

Gibson, R. C. "Reconceptualizing Retirement for Black Americans." In E. P. Stoller and R. C. Campbell (eds.), *Worlds of Difference.* Thousand Oaks, Calif.: Sage, 1994.

Giltian, J. M. "Using Life Review to Facilitate Self-actualization in Elderly Women." *Gerontology and Geriatrics Education,* 1990, *10* (4), 75–83.

Greenberg, R. M. *Education for Older Adult Learning: Annotated Bibliography.* New York: Greenwood Press, 1993.

Gubrium, J. F. *Speaking of Life: Horizons of Meaning for Nursing Home Residents.* New York: Aldine de Gruyter, 1993.

Gutmann, D. L. "An Exploration of Ego Configurations in Middle and Later Life." In B. L. Neugarten (ed.), *Personality in Middle and Late Life: Empirical Studies.* New York: Atherton Press, 1964.

Gutmann, D. L "Parenthood: A Key to the Comparative Study of the Life Cycle." In N. Datan and L. Ginsberg (eds.), *Life-Span Developmental Psychology: Normative Life Crises.* New York: Simon & Schuster, 1975.

Gutmann, D. L. *Reclaimed Powers.* New York: Basic Books, 1987.

Haight, B. K., and Webster, J. D. (eds.). *The Art and Science of Reminiscing.* Washington, D.C.: Taylor & Francis, 1995.

Hasselkus, B. R. "Patient Education and the Elderly." *Physical & Occupational Therapy in Geriatrics*, 1983, 2 (3), 55–70.

Hiemstra, R. "Lifelong Education and Personal Growth." In A. Monk (ed.), *The Columbia Retirement Handbook*. New York: Columbia University Press, 1994.

Holahan, C. K. "Women's Goal Orientations Across the Life Cycle: Findings from the Terman Study of the Gifted." In B. F. Turner and L. E. Troll (eds.), *Women Growing Older: Psychological Perspectives*. Thousand Oaks, Calif.: Sage, 1994.

Hudson, F. M. *The Adult Years: Mastering the Art of Self-Renewal*. San Francisco: Jossey-Bass, 1991.

Huyck, M. H. "The Relevance of Psychodynamic Theories for Understanding Gender Among Older Women." In B. F. Turner and L. E. Troll (eds.), *Women Growing Older*. Thousand Oaks, Calif.: Sage, 1994.

Josselson, R., and Lieblich, A. (eds.). *Interpreting Experience: The Narrative Study of Lives*. Thousand Oaks: Sage, 1995.

Kaminsky, M. (ed.). *The Uses of Reminiscence*. New York: Haworth Press, 1984.

Kaminsky, M. "The Arts and Social Work: Writing and Reminiscing in Old Age: Voices from Within the Process." *Journal of Gerontological Social Work*, 1985, 8 (3–4), 225–246.

Kidder, T. *Old Friends*. New York: Houghton Mifflin, 1993.

Kivnick, H. Q. "Everyday Mental Health: A Guide to Assessing Life Strengths." *Generations*, 1993, 17 (4), 13–20.

Kreitlow, D. J., and Kreitlow, B. W. "Careers After 60: Choices in Retirement." *Adult Learning*, 1989, 1 (3), 10–13.

Labouvie-Vief, G. "Adaptive Dimensions of Adult Cognition." In N. Datan and N. Lohmann (eds.), *Transitions of Aging*. New York: Academic Press, 1980.

Labouvie-Vief, G. "Models of Cognitive Functioning in the Older Adult: Research Needs in Educational Gerontology." In R. H. Sherron and D. B. Lumsden (eds.), *Introduction to Educational Gerontology*. (3rd ed.) New York: Hemisphere, 1990a.

Labouvie-Vief, G. "Neo-Piagetian Perspective on Adult Cognitive Development." In R. J. Sternberg and C. A. Berg (eds.), *Intellectual Development*. Cambridge, England: Cambridge University Press, 1990b.

Lamdin, L., and Fugate, M. *Elderlearning: New Frontier in an Aging Society*. Phoenix, Ariz.: Oryx Press, 1997.

Langer, E. J., and Rodin, J. "The Effects of Choice and Enhanced Personal Responsibility: A Field Experience in an Institutional Setting. *Journal of Personality and Social Psychology*, 1977, 34, 191–198.

Light, L. "Interactions Between Memory and Language in Old Age." In J.E. Birren and K. W. Schaie (eds.), *Handbook of the Psychology of Aging*. (3rd ed.) New York: Academic Press, 1990.

Lindbloom, E. "America's Aging Population: Changing the Face of Health Care." *Journal of the American Medical Association*, February 3, 1993, 269 (5), 674–675.

Long, H. B. "Self-Directed Learning by the Elderly: A Review of Dissertation Abstracts, 1966–1991." *Educational Gerontology*, 1993, 19 (1), 1–7.

Lyman, A. J., and Edwards, M. E. "Reminiscence Poetry Groups: Sheepherding—A Navajo Cultural Tie That Binds." *Activities, Adaptation, and Aging*, 1989, 13 (4), 1–8.

Maas, H. S., and Kuypers, J. A. *From Thirty to Seventy*. San Francisco: Jossey-Bass, 1977.

Magee, J. J. *A Professional's Guide to Older Adults' Life Review: Releasing the Peace Within*. Lexington, Mass.: Lexington Books, 1988a.

Magee, J. J. "Using Poetry as an Aid to Life Review." *Activities, Adaptation, and Aging*, 1988b, 12 (1–2), 91–101.

Manheimer, R. J. "Creative Retirement in an Aging Society." In R. B. Fischer, M. L. Blazey, and H. T. Lipman (eds.), *Students of the Third Age*. New York: Macmillan, 1992.

Manheimer, R. J., and Snodgrass, D. "New Roles and Norms for Older Adults Through Higher Education." *Educational Gerontology*, 1993, 19, 585–595.

Maslow, A. *Motivation and Personality*. (2nd ed.) New York: Harper & Row, 1970.

McMahon, A. W., and Rhudick, P. J. "Reminiscing in the Aged: An Adaptational Response." In S. Lewin and R. U. Kahana (eds.), *Psychodynamic Studies on Aging: Creativity, Reminiscing and Dying.* New York: International Universities Press, 1967.

Merriam, S. B. "Reminiscence and Life Review: The Potential for Educational Intervention." In R. H. Sherron and D. B. Lumsden (eds.), *Introduction to Educational Gerontology.* (3rd ed.) New York: Hemisphere, 1990.

Moody, H. R. "Reminiscence and the Recovery of the Public World." In M. Kaminsky (ed.), *The Uses of Reminiscence: New Ways of Working with Older Adults.* New York: Haworth Press, 1984.

Moody, H. R. *Abundance of Life: Human Development Policies for an Aging Society.* New York: Columbia University Press, 1988a.

Moody, H. R. "Twenty-Five Years of the Life Review: Where Did We Come From? Where Are We Going?" *Journal of Gerontological Social Work,* 1988b, *12* (3–4), 7–21.

Myerhoff, B. In M. Kaminsky (ed.). *Remembered Lives: The Work of Ritual Storytelling and Growing Older.* Ann Arbor: University of Michigan Press, 1992.

Neugarten, B. L. *The Meanings of Age.* Chicago: University of Chicago Press, 1996.

North Carolina Center for Creative Retirement. *College for Seniors.* Asheville, N.C.: University of North Carolina at Asheville, 1994.

Peck, R. C. "Psychological Developments in the Second Half of Life." In B. L. Neugarten (ed.), *Middle Age and Aging.* Chicago: University of Chicago Press, 1968.

Perlstein, S. *A Stage for Memory: Life History Plays by Older Adults.* The Work of the Hodson Senior Center Drama Group. New York: Teachers and Writers Collaborative, 1981.

Perlstein, S. "Transformation: Life Review and Communal Theater." *Journal of Gerontological Social Work,* 1988, *12* (3–4), 137–148.

Peterson, C., Vaillant, G. E., and Seligman, M.E.P. "Pessimistic Explanatory Style Is a Risk Factor for Physical Illness: A Thirty-Five-Year Longitudinal Study." *Journal of Personality and Social Psychology,* 1988, *55* (1), 23–25.

Piskurich, G. M. *Self-Directed Learning: A Practical Guide to Design, Development, and Implementation.* San Francisco: Jossey-Bass, 1993.

Reingold, E., and Werby, E. "Supporting the Independence of Elderly Residents Through Control over Their Environment." *Journal of Housing for the Elderly,* 1990, 7–8, pp. 25–32.

Rodin, J., and Langer, E. J. (1977). "Long-Term Effects of a Control-Relevant Intervention with the Institutionalized Aged." *Journal of Personality and Social Psychology,* 1977, *35,* 897–902.

Rodin, J., Schooler, C., and Schaie, K. W. (eds.) *Self-Directedness: Cause and Effects Throughout the Life Course.* Hillsdale, N.J.: Lawrence Erlbaum, 1990.

Rowe, J. W., and Kahn, R. L. "Human Aging: Usual and Successful." *Science,* 1987, *237* (4811), 143–149. (EJ 356 053)

Ryff, C. D., and Essex, M. J. "The Interpretation of Life Experience and Well-Being: The Sample Case of Relocation." *Psychology and Aging,* 1992, *4,* 507–517.

Schaie, K. W. "Variability in Cognitive Function in the Elderly: Implications for Societal Participation." In A. Woodhead, M. Bender, and R. Leonard (eds.), *Phenotypic Variation in Populations: Relevance to Risk Management.* New York: Plenum, 1988.

Schaie, K. W. "The Optimization of Cognitive Functioning in Old Age: Predictions Based on Cohort-Sequential and Longitudinal Data." In P. B. Baltes and M. M. Baltes (eds.), *Successful Aging: Perspectives from the Behavioral Sciences.* London: Cambridge University, 1989.

Schaie, K. W. "Intellectual Development in Adulthood." In J. E. Birren and K. W. Schaie (eds.), *Handbook of the Psychology of Aging.* (3rd ed.) New York: Academic Press, 1990.

Schaie, K. W., and Willis, S. L. "Can Decline in Adult Intellectual Functioning Be Reversed?" *Developmental Psychology,* 1986, *2, 223–232.

Schaie, K. W., and Willis, S. L. *Adult Development and Aging.* (4th ed.) New York: HarperCollins, 1996.

Shuldiner, D. "The Older Student of Humanities: The Seeker and the Source." In T. R. Cole, D. D. Van Tassel, and R. Kastenbaum (eds.), *Handbook of the Humanities and Aging.* New York: Springer, 1992.

Simonton, D. K. "Creativity and Wisdom in Aging." In J. E. Birren and K. W. Schaie (eds.), *Handbook of the Psychology of Aging.* (3rd ed.) New York: Academic Press, 1990.

Solomon, D. H., and others. *A Consumer's Guide to Aging.* Baltimore: Johns Hopkins, 1992.

Syme, S. L. "Control and Health: An Epidemiological Perspective." In J. Rodin, C. Schooler, and K. W. Schaie (eds.), *Self-Directedness: Cause and Effects Throughout the Life Course.* Hillsdale, N.J.: Lawrence Erlbaum, 1990.

Turner, B. F., and Troll, L. E. (eds.). *Women Growing Older, Psychological Perspectives.* Thousand Oaks, Calif.: Sage, 1994.

Vaillant, G. E. *The Wisdom of the Ego.* Cambridge, Mass.: Harvard University Press, 1993.

Vaillant, G. E. *Adaptation to Life.* Cambridge, Mass.: Harvard University Press, 1995.

Vaillant, G. E. "Adult Development: Reality or Fantasy." Lectures to the Cape Cod Institute, Albert Einstein College of Medicine, Eastham, Mass., July 28–August 1, 1997.

Vaillant, G. E., and Vaillant, C. O. "Natural History of Male Psychological Health, XII: A 45-Year Study of Predictors of Successful Aging at Age 65." *American Journal of Psychiatry,* 1990, *147* (1), 31–37.

Walker, J. (ed.). *Changing Concepts of Retirement: Educational Implications.* Brookfield, Vt.: Arena, Ashgate, 1996.

Wolf, M. A. "The Meaning of Education in Late Life." *Geriatrics and Education,* 1985, 5 (3), 51–59.

Wolf, M. A. "Older Adults and Reminiscence in the Classroom." *Adult Learning,* 1992a, 3 (8), 19–21.

Wolf, M. A. "Personal Development Through Learning in Later Life." In L. A. Cavaliere and A. Sgroi (eds.), *Learning for Personal Development.* New Directions for Adult and Continuing Education, no. 53. San Francisco: Jossey-Bass, 1992b.

Wolf, M. A. *Older Adults: Learning in the Third Age.* Columbus, Ohio: ERIC Clearinghouse on Adult, Career, and Vocational Education, 1994. (Information Series No. 358)

Wolf, M. A., and Leahy, M. A. (eds.). *Adults in Transition.* Washington, D.C.: American Association for Adult and Continuing Education, in press.

MARY ALICE WOLF is professor of human development and gerontology and director of the Institute in Gerontology at Saint Joseph College, West Hartford, Connecticut.

Research findings describe the cognitive capability of older adults, their participation in a range of educational activities, their response to instructional approaches, and their reflection about their own learning. These findings combine to emphasize the importance of contextual and environmental factors, including educational programs, in understanding how older adults use learning to meet the challenges confronting them.

Major Streams of Research Probing Older Adult Learning

James C. Fisher

Many factors combine to call attention to the increasing importance of learning for coping, enjoyment, employment, and for influencing and contributing to society. These include increases in the number of older adults, in their proportion to the total population, in their average life expectancy, in their average educational attainment, and increases in the age at which social security will be provided to their younger cohorts. These increases, combined with retirement at earlier ages, cause uncertainty about the availability of certain retirement benefits as well as provide for greater career and leisure opportunities.

The purpose of this chapter is to enhance our understanding of the processes by which learning assists in meeting the challenges of older adulthood. This chapter highlights major findings about the facilitation of older adult learning gathered from journal articles, books, and dissertations published during the past decade. Comprehensive reviews of research on this topic have been published by Peterson (1983), Lumsden (1985), and Sherron and Lumsden (1990). Manheimer, Snodgrass, and Moskow-McKenzie (1995); Bass (1995); and Fischer, Blazey, and Lipman (1992) have combined findings from research on older adult learning with discussions of particular program and policy emphases.

Research by its very nature is incremental, and not inclined toward innovative directions and daring initiatives; it builds progressively on earlier studies as part of a continuing process in which findings are replicated, refined, and used as stepping stones for what follows. Research is also a reductive process. The broad heterogeneity of the older adult population and the distinctiveness of individuals often fail to surface amid generalizations about older adults as a homogeneous group. Fisher (1993) and others have underscored

NEW DIRECTIONS FOR ADULT AND CONTINUING EDUCATION, no. 77, Spring 1998 © Jossey-Bass Publishers

the importance of viewing older adulthood from the perspective of developmental periods rather than as a single time frame or on the basis of chronological age.

This chapter is divided into sections describing research on cognition and memory, participation, instructional processes, literacy, and reflection on learning, generalizing about those findings with practical application.

The Cognitive Framework

Most inquiry into the cognition of older adults centers around the search for a theoretical construct that describes the precise nature and cause of age-related change. Many research questions are framed by larger issues, such as the respective impact of biology and environment on age-related cognition, the utility of cross-sectional and longitudinal analyses, or the appropriateness of examining the amount of information processed versus the particular tasks being performed.

Cognitive Change. Whereas the purpose of earlier generations of research may have been to measure decrements attributable to the aging process, most current research is interested in discovering the shape of cognitive change. Age-related decrements notwithstanding, psychological research among older adults recognizes that normal aging does not usually cause a simultaneous decline in all cognitive functions, that there are wide individual differences in the onset and pattern of cognitive change, and that although "some functions decline, others remain stable, and others even improve" across the life span (Schacter, Kihlstrom, Kaszniak, and Valdiserri, 1993, p. 327). Willis claims that recent studies have presented too pessimistic a view of the cognitive capabilities of older adults: "their level of cognitive functioning may be more substantial than previously assumed or demonstrated" (1990, p. 877).

In his landmark Seattle Longitudinal Study, Schaie verified that decrements in cognitive ability "cannot be reliably confirmed prior to age 60 (except for word fluency) . . . [and are] indeed found for all abilities by age 67" (1994, p. 308). But these decrements occur at a modest level and in "stair-step" patterns until age 80, with fewer than half of all observed individuals at age 81 showing reliable decrements after age 74 (Schaie, 1994, p. 308). Lohman and Scheurman (1992, p. 87) note that abilities that show decline in the later adult years tend to feature perceptual speed or the ability to solve novel problems, both indicators of decline in fluid intelligence. Walsh and Hershey (1993, p. 580) attest to the efficiency of experts and older adults in their use of information to solve financial planning problems, providing evidence that age-related decrements in some basic cognitive processes may not translate into decrements in everyday complex problem-solving performance. Giambra (1993, p. 269) concludes that older adults sustain attention as well as young adults do for long periods of time.

Noncognitive Factors. Of particular import for adult educators is the impact of noncognitive, or environmental, factors on cognition, These factors result from education, professional and personal experiences, and lifestyle choices. Fry writes that "the intellectual abilities and learning effectiveness of older persons are not merely genetically programmed, but are influenced by exogenous factors such as self-knowledge, motivation and expectancies" (1992, p. 305).

Schaie (1994, p. 311) describes the following variables as providing positive influences on cognition: the absence of cardiovascular and other chronic diseases; living in favorable environmental circumstances; having above-average education and a history of occupational pursuits involving high complexity and low routine; living on above-average income in an intact family; and involvement in activities typically available in complex and intellectually stimulating environments. He also identifies a flexible personality at middle age, marriage to a spouse with high cognitive status, maintenance of high levels of perceptual processing speed into old age, satisfaction with one's accomplishments in midlife and early old age, and recent participation in educative activity as variables that reduce the risk of cognitive decline in old age.

Another perspective on environmental influence views cognitive deficits as the consequence of undemanding intellectual environments (Baron and Cerella, 1993, p. 175). This view assumes that the environments to which older adults are currently exposed fail to support the intensive cognitive activity that characterized earlier stages of educational and career development. Research findings provide support for the contention that disuse can make a significant contribution to age differences in cognitive performances. Kasworm and Medina support this notion with the finding that "everyday life task performance of a subgroup of functional literacy knowledge and skills appears to not be significantly affected by possible 'diminishment' of a general capacity in aging adults" (1990, p. 44).

The impact of activity extends beyond that which is educative in only the cognitive sense: findings have also demonstrated that peripheral nervous system function can be preserved at a relatively high level among older individuals who have kept fit through systematic exercise, and can be restored to varying degrees among elderly persons whose fitness levels have been improved by participation in an exercise program (Bashore and Goddard, 1993, p. 205).

Training Interventions. A second finding significant for adult educators comes from those studies examining outcomes of remedial training interventions on persons with declines in fluid abilities. Characteristics of learning tasks most associated with a decline in fluid intelligence are those that are fast paced, present problem-solving situations not based on past experience, or deal with associative memory and memory-span loss. They provide evidence that, given appropriate reinforcement and support, loss in cognitive performance may be reversible, and such declines may be restored (Willis, 1990; Fry, 1992).

Significant improvement through training was found in many of the studies. Some found that the training effect continued up to several years after the intervention. For older adults experiencing previous age-related decline, training effects reflected some level of remediation. For those whose functioning has remained stable from earlier years, training effects resulted in improvement above prior performance. According to Willis (1990), the emphasis has shifted from probing whether performance can be improved by interventions to discovering the nature of the training gain and the conditions under which it occurs.

However, others urge caution: Hayslip (1989), for example, questions the assumption of a unidimensional understanding of fluid intelligence. He suggests that greater attention be given to the multidimensional nature of aging, the salience of individual differences in performing intellectual and problem-solving tasks, and the broad range of cognitive and noncognitive influences that bear on intellectual functioning in later life.

Memory

Greater sensitivity exists and more problems are reported with memory deficits than with any other facet of cognition. Although a general consensus exists that some decline in memory performance may be associated with normal aging, there is a divergence about its exact nature. The study of memory parallels the study of cognition among older adults in that careful examination reveals a pattern "in which some functions may have declined while others are preserved more or less intact" (Schacter, Kihlstrom, Kaszniak, and Valdiserri, 1993, p. 328). Recent memory research has focused on three general areas: the nature of the loss, noncognitive factors that influence it, and strategies that may contribute to effective memory usage.

The Nature of the Memory Loss. Many studies examine various stages in the memory process to identify those elements that contribute to age-related memory failure and preservation. In the effort to locate the problem, several findings emerge: memory as an integral component of the cognitive process is most generally affected by a person's level of intellectual and other cognitive abilities; in fact, these multiple abilities are more predictive of performance on a variety of memory tasks than are the effects of age (Hultsch and Dixon, 1990, p. 266; Chambliss, 1994). Salthouse (1993) and others have shown that perceptual speed accounts for a significant portion of the age-related variance in memory performance (Smith, 1996, p. 242). Differences in performance attributable to age occur in some forms of memory usage but not in others. For example, findings indicate that older adults may perform poorly on explicit memory tasks, such as recall and recognition, but their performance on implicit memory tasks, such as word-stem or word-fragment completion, is unaffected. Similarly, prospective memory (remembering to execute planned actions) has been shown to be much less impaired by age than retrospective memory (recalling or recognizing information previously presented) (Maylor, 1993, p. 547).

The search for location leads to investigation whether the problem lies with the acquisition, retention, or retrieval process. Youngjohn and Crook (1993) found virtually no forgetting of material already acquired into memory at any age, and they concluded that memory deficits occur in both acquisition and retrieval, but that retention remains relatively stable across the adult life span. In general, research findings are replete with contradictory conclusions about the function of working memory and its components.

Noncognitive Factors in Memory Loss. The second broad area receiving scrutiny is the identification of noncognitive or environmental factors that impact memory preservation or deficit. These include personality traits (such as flexibility or introversion), acculturation, motivation, practice in performing memory tasks, appropriate and efficient use of cognitive strategies, and social activity and affective processes. Indeed, those who simply felt younger than their chronological age were able to recall significantly more material than those who felt their age or older (Montgomery, 1995).

Among the more influential environmental factors impacting memory usage are negative emotional states, usually associated with anxiety, depression, or withdrawal. Deptula, Singh, and Pomara (1993, p. 433) concluded that among the elderly, higher levels of negative affective states were associated with poorer memory, and that the elderly are more vulnerable to the adverse effects of negative emotional states on memory than the young. In contrast, Chambliss (1994) reported that level of depression affected the number of memory complaints rather than memory performance, but that age did not have an effect on the number of memory complaints. Dellefield and McDougall (1996) found that persons with depression had lower memory self-efficacy scores, but that depression resulted in no difference on memory performance. Researchers caution that these findings do not necessarily imply that one's emotional state affects memory; it is possible that poorer memory functioning causes some persons to be more anxious and depressed (Deptula, Singh, and Pomara, 1993).

Another important noncognitive factor influencing memory loss is the perception by older adults that they possess a low level of memory-related self-efficacy and control, and these, together with inappropriate performance attributions, result in lowered effort and poor performance. According to Hultsch and Dixon (1990, p. 268), this view of memory self-efficacy is receiving more support, although it is increasingly apparent that the interface between cognitive and social processes is a complex one.

Strategies for Effective Memory Usage. A third direction in memory research is the identification of strategies that contribute to effective memory use. Various studies found that, in everyday tasks, older adults are more likely to use external memory strategies (lists, notes, places, persons, calendars) than internal memory strategies (rehearsal, elaboration, effort) (McDougall, 1995). Learning behavioral relaxation techniques has been used to improve the memory. Although studies depict mixed results from memory instruction, Greenberg and Powers (1987, p. 263) suggest that slowing the pace of learning, giving encouragement to learners to organize memory items, providing training in the use of imagery and mnemonics, and giving information about normal age-related memory changes have resulted in improved memory performance.

Implications for Practice

Educators of older persons may be encouraged by the increasingly positive view of their cognitive capability and challenged by variable patterns of individual cognitive development. Many older adults are able and highly self-directed learners with ample educational and intellectual resources available to them, but others could benefit from assistance in developing strategies to assist cognition and memory.

Many general strategies are drawn from adult education literature:

- Develop a supportive climate.
- Emphasize abilities rather than disabilities.
- Allow for individual pacing of instruction.
- Use materials that are socially and culturally relevant.
- Provide timely and meaningful feedback.
- Structure activities to allow for learner flexibility to use varied and preferred visual resources (Fry, 1992).

Another strategy follows a cognitivist approach: educators can clarify the structure of the material to be learned; encourage older adult learners to persist in their learning by providing questions, prompts, organizers, or directions; and guide the learner's attention and strengthen the connection between current and new information (although findings are divided on the effectiveness of advance organizers and questions). Practitioners might also help adult learners diagnose their current understanding of a new problem situation and build on relevant areas of understanding and competence. Literature-based studies by Glass (1996) and Twitchell, Cherry, and Trott (1996) provide theory-grounded strategies for assisting older adult learners.

Yet another approach focuses on basic restructuring activities: Fry (1992, p. 316) claims that approaches to learning used by older adults often rely on ineffective problem-solving concepts and strategies effective in the past instead of generating new approaches. One example is to expand and refine the older adult's repertoire of crystallized abilities to compensate for slowed fluid activities.

Participation in Learning Activities

Data published by the National Center for Education Statistics (NCES) from the 1991 National Household Education Survey (NHES) (Kopka and Peng, 1993) indicate that 17.2 percent of persons aged 60 to 64 and 10.5 percent of persons 65 years of age and older participate in adult education. In the 60-to-64 age group, main reasons given for participating in education are to improve or advance in a job (9 percent) or for personal/family/social reasons (7.4 percent). In the group 65 years and older, the main reasons given are for personal/family/social reasons (7.6 percent) and to improve or advance in a job

(2.3 percent). For both age groups, training for a new job, improving basic skills, or obtaining a diploma or degree were given as the reasons for participation by less than 1 percent of the respondents. Data from the 1994–1995 National Household Education Survey (Stowe, 1996) indicate that whereas 2.25 percent of persons age 65 and over participated in a work-related course, 13.47 percent participated in a course for personal development. These and other sources indicate that although the dominant reason for participation is personal and social enrichment, a significant portion of older persons are still engaged in work-related education.

Job-related learning was examined further by NCES and by Peterson and Wendt (1995). From the 1991 National Household Education Survey data base (Kopka and Peng, 1994), 28.5 percent of employed persons age 55 to 64 years and 16.5 percent of those 65 years of age and over took at least one employment-related training course during the previous year. Peterson and Wendt (1995), using data gathered by Lou Harris and Associates, report 30 percent of those 55 to 59, 26 percent age 60 to 64, 21 percent age 65 to 69, 15 percent age 70 to 74, and 10 percent age 75 and older answered "Yes" to the question, "Since your fiftieth birthday, have you taken any kind of courses or training specifically to improve your job skills or employment opportunities?" In interpreting these data, Peterson and Wendt call our attention to the renewed need for older adults to improve work-related skills through education, training, or both because of the absence of corporate pension programs for half of all retirees and the dramatic expansion of knowledge through technology. Participant expectations included positive outcomes such as improvement in work effectiveness and an increase in job longevity. Major barriers cited were cost, lack of confidence in one's ability, low likelihood of getting a better job, and lack of transportation. Nevertheless, age and prior education are still the most important variables in predicting participation in work-related education by older persons.

Several studies investigated older adult students' reasons for attending college. Butler (1992) learned that intrinsic reasons and interest in the humanities and liberal arts explained his sample's motivation. O'Connor (1987) discovered that older college students face the same major barriers as middle-aged students—lack of time and the cost of tuition—but that older students enrolled because they enjoyed learning for its own sake, and they were similar to Elderhostel students their own age, from a motivational perspective. In a college-based Learning-in-Retirement (LIR) program, Bynum (1992) described the underlying motivational orientations as self-actualization, perceived cognitive gaps, intellectual curiosity, and social contact. He also found that participation in LIR programs confirmed the continuity theory of aging, that older adult students' involvement in educational activities represented a continuation of similar activities from earlier life stages. Bankhead (1996) also learned that, among students in computer literacy courses, participation was influenced by factors that had their origins in earlier life stages as well as by factors such as practical need, the priority of other interests, the desire to keep up to date, perceptions about technology, and the influence of family members. From the perspective of the sponsoring institution, Martin (1995) found that LIR programs could foster the loyalty of older adult students by conscious institutional efforts at building relationships with the older students, commitment to understanding their educational needs, efforts to assist in their continuing interest in learning, and opportunities for older students to take an active role in other areas of campus life.

In her study of elderly women, Morris (1995) concluded that they learned to use assistive technology in order to enhance those skills required to live alone; this allowed them to maintain their freedom to reject family help and continue their pursuit of familiar social roles. Hammond (1992) found that older learners were motivated to participate in Sunday school by their desire to fulfill social and psychological needs, especially coping and expressive needs, and to learn from their peers.

Three studies used McClusky's "theory of margin" (see Hiemstra, Chapter One, this volume) as a theoretical framework to aid in understanding the motives and needs of older learners. Wolfe (1990) learned that participation in an LIR program enabled older students to age more successfully by increasing their resources, thus correlating educational and social gains with participation. Examining strategies used in negotiating the retirement transition, Adair and Mowsesian (1993) also found that learning through formal and informal contexts increased individual power by meeting needs and goals associated with managing and controlling individual load, thereby maintaining a person's sense of well-being and autonomy. Hanson (1988) identified three motivational themes—survival, social, and self-development—and observed that participants were influenced by both deficit and growth incentives. She found that initial participation is often the result of a perceived deficit, but continued participation requires a growth orientation.

Sears (1989) examined the number of self-directed learning projects undertaken by older adults together with the motivational factors and benefits resulting from these learning activities. Subjects averaged 1.99 self-directed learning projects per person in the previous year, and 90 percent reported conducting at least one learning project in the past year. The main incentive was self-fulfillment and enjoyment; major obstacles were time, cost, other responsibilities, deciding what to learn, remembering new material or information, and poor health.

Instructional Processes

Among studies focusing on the instructional process, Dubes (1987) compared the effectiveness of lecture, structured discussion, and guided poster sessions as teaching modes at nutrition sites and concluded that although posttest scores for all three modes were higher than pretest scores, the poster mode resulted in greater amounts of retained learning than the other two. In examining the processes by which older adults acquire computer and word processing skills, Rich (1993) found that pedagogical learning methods were appropriate for this purpose because they responded to the needs of older adults for a high level of teacher direction and structure at the introductory level of training. These students favored small age-segregated classes with teacher-directed instruction, written directions, and other material they could review at home as preferred instructional aids. Contrary to andragogical assumptions, the study found that older adult computer learners neither wanted nor expected a role in the planning of their learning, and that application of past experience with typing or with computers resulted in more negative than positive instances of transfer of learning.

Literacy

Data from the 1992 National Adult Literacy Survey (Brown, Prisuta, Jacobs, and Campbell, 1996) indicate that 71 percent of adults age 60 and older demonstrate limited prose skills, 68 percent have difficulty finding and processing quantitative information in printed materials, and 80 percent demonstrate limited document literacy skills. The researchers found that higher levels of literacy proficiencies existed among older adults who had higher educational level, had higher income levels, or were either employed or volunteers in retirement. Many of the respondents surveyed reported receiving help from family or friends with basic literacy tasks, although the number needing such help was judged much larger than the number reporting assistance.

Fisher (1990) found that the use of functional literacy skills among nursing home residents was influenced by their level of skill and comprehension, their physical ability, their perceived need, and their prior experience. Those who described themselves as readers used literacy for expressive purposes, and those who described themselves as nonreaders regarded reading as useful mainly for instrumental purposes. Kasworm and Medina (1989) linked the viability of literacy in the senior years with a person's frame of reference, social context, self-education activities, and life context.

Reflections on Learning

A number of researchers asked older adults to reflect on various experiences of learning. In probing how older adults learned from experience, Logsdail (1990) found that relationships with others and relationship with self were the two most discussed value perspectives. However, insight gained through relationships with others was described primarily in a childhood context, whereas insight gained from within the self was depicted as an adult activity. Learning from within the self included adjusting to changing life circumstances, persevering toward one's goals, learning from past successes and mistakes, introspection, and faith as a reinforcement of self. Logsdail (1990) concluded that insight from life experience resulted in a level of self-understanding that served as the foundation for negotiating the course of older adulthood.

In an inquiry into how a group of women learned great-grandmothering, Reese (1994) found that their learning was often tacit, gained from their own experience, and mediated through a female of the birth family. Learning took the form of both social learning (mediated, personal, and tacit learning) and goal-directed learning (explicit, self-directed learning).

Brown (1995) probed the process by which older adults changed their views of themselves from smokers to nonsmokers: it included handling ambivalence, feeling pride, integrating responses from family and friends, reconfirming their earlier decision to stop smoking, and maintaining a hope of success.

Michael (1991) identified elements of a learning process practiced by a group of older adults as building on experience, organizing material, evaluating information, relating information to situations, and using information to make decisions. Their resources included a variety of networks, a variety of materials, and expert advice.

Merriam's "Constructed Uses of Reminiscence Scale" (1993) resulted in the identification of three primary uses of reminiscence: therapeutic (coping with life's problems, understanding oneself), informative (storytelling, transmission of educational or cultural material, passing on the values or lessons from the past), and enjoyment (reliving pleasant experiences, lifting spirits), with the conclusion that reminiscence provides the means for facilitating late-life growth and development.

Conclusion

It is impossible to capture both the scope and detail of the research addressing older adult learning in a few pages. This body of knowledge is contained in various kinds of publications across several disciplines. It is based on both longitudinal and cross-sectional research, on quantitative and qualitative analyses, and on large and small numbers of subjects. It includes both laboratory and community-based research, studies where context and environment are disregarded, and studies that are entirely context-specific.

This chapter has focused on research of interest to educators who work with or study older adults. It endeavors to reflect some of the shifts in research emphasis as well as specify areas where practitioner impact on older adult learning could be most powerful.

What might we hope such a review of research will reveal in another decade? While the laboratory research on cognition and memory provides significant contributions to our understanding of older adult learning, we might hope for a greater move from the laboratory to the community. Since research follows available instruments and methodologies, such a move would mean the development of improved measures for understanding the role of noncognitive factors in the learning process.

The findings suggest that context is important in our understanding of learning by older adults. Yet contexts that appeared in the studies lacked the heterogeneity of the older adult experience. Many of them described specific experiences: great-grandmothering, avoiding dependency, Sunday school, Learning-in-Retirement. But there was little discussion of the learning by older adults whose experiences rendered them socially, culturally, economically, or educationally disadvantaged. Nor was there a linkage between developmental stages of older adulthood and learning. We might hope for both a continued emphasis on the environment of learning and attention especially to the diversity of racial-ethnic, socio-cultural, and psychological contexts represented in the older adult experience.

Finally, we might hope for additional findings that provide reason for optimism about the capability of older adults to learn, about the efficacy of programs to address their learning needs and facilitate their growth, and about the propensity of older adults to rely upon learning—self-directed, informal, and formal—to meet the challenges they face.

References

Adair, S. R., and Mowsesian, R. "The Meanings and Motivations of Learning During the Retirement Transition." *Educational Gerontology,* 1993, *19* (4), 317–330.

Bankhead, D. R. "Older Adults and Computer Courses: Preadult, Adult, and Contemporary Factors in Participation." Unpublished doctoral dissertation, University of Georgia, 1996.

Baron, A., and Cerella, J. "Laboratory Tests of the Disuse Account of Cognitive Decline." In J. Cerella, J. Rybash, W. Hoyer, and M. L. Commons (eds.), *Adult Information Processing: Limits on Loss.* San Diego: Academic Press, 1993.

Bashore, T. R., and Goddard, P. H. "Preservative and Restorative Effects of Aerobic Fitness on the Age-Related Slowing of Mental Processing Speed." In J. Cerella, J. Rybash, W. Hoyer, and M. L. Commons (eds.), *Adult Information Processing: Limits on Loss.* San Diego: Academic Press, 1993.

Bass, S. A. (ed.). *Older and Active: How Americans over 55 Are Contributing to Society.* New Haven, Conn.: Yale University, 1995.

Brown, H., Prisuta, R., Jacobs, B., and Campbell, A. *Statistical Analysis Report: Literacy of Older Adults in America.* Washington, D.C.: National Center for Education Statistics, 1996.

Brown, J. M. "Redefining Smoking and the Self as a Nonsmoker: A Study of Smoking Cessation in Older Adults." Unpublished doctoral dissertation, University of Wisconsin–Milwaukee, 1995.

Butler, D. Q. "A Comparative Study of Older Adult College Student and Faculty Opinions of Learning Factors." Unpublished doctoral dissertation, University of New Orleans, 1992.

Bynum, L. L. "Motivations of Third-Age Students in Learning-in-Retirement Institutes." Unpublished doctoral dissertation, University of South Carolina, 1992.

Chambliss, L. N. "The Relationships Between Learning Efficiency, Memory Complaints, and Objective Test Results in Different Age Groups." Unpublished doctoral dissertation, University of Tennessee, 1994.

Dellefield, K. S., and McDougall, G. J. "Increasing Metamemory in Older Adults." *Nursing Research,* 1996, *45* (5), 284–290.

Deptula, D., Singh, R., and Pomara, N. "Aging, Emotional States, and Memory." *American Journal of Psychiatry,* 1993, *150* (3), 429–434.

Dubes, M. J. "Comparisons of Lecture, Discussion, and Poster Modes of Instruction of Adults Ages 59 to 90 Attending Nutrition Sites." Unpublished doctoral dissertation, University of Nebraska–Lincoln, 1987.

Fischer, R. B., Blazey, M. L., and Lipman, H. T. *Students of the Third Age.* New York: Macmillan, 1992.

Fisher, J. C. "The Function of Literacy in a Nursing Home Context." *Educational Gerontology,* 1990, *16* (1), 105–116.

Fisher, J. C. "A Framework for Describing Developmental Change Among Older Adults." *Adult Education Quarterly,* 1993, *43* (2), 76–89.

Fry, P. S. "A Consideration of Cognitive Factors in the Learning and Education of Older Adults." *International Review of Education,* 1992, *38* (4), 303–325.

Giambra, L. M. "Sustained Attention in Older Adults: Performance and Processes." In J. Cerella, J. Rybash, W. Hoyer, and M. L. Commons (eds.). *Adult Information Processing: Limits on Loss.* San Diego: Academic Press, 1993.

Glass, J. C. "Factors Affecting Learning in Older Adults." *Educational Gerontology,* 1996, *22* (4), 359–372.

Greenberg, C., and Powers, S. M. "Memory Improvement Among Adult Learners." *Educational Gerontology,* 1987, *13* (3), 263–280.

Hammond, J. T. "The Facilitation of Older Adult Learning in Local Church Educational Programs: The Case of the Sunday School." Unpublished doctoral dissertation, North Carolina State University, 1992.

Hanson, A. L. H. "A Model of Deficit/Growth Motives and Learning Needs of Older Participants." Unpublished doctoral dissertation, University of Oklahoma, 1988.

Hayslip, B. "Fluid Ability Training with Aged People: A Past with a Future?" *Educational Gerontology,* 1989, *15* (6), 573–595.

Hultsch, D. F., and Dixon, R. A. "Learning and Memory in Aging." In J. E. Birren and K. W. Schaie (eds.), *Handbook of the Psychology of Aging* (3rd ed.). San Diego: Academic Press, 1990.

Kasworm, C. E., and Medina, R. A. "Perspectives of Literacy in the Senior Adult Years." *Educational Gerontology,* 1989, *15* (1), 65–79.

Kasworm, C. E., and Medina, R. A. "Adult Competence in Everyday Tasks: A Cross-Sectional Secondary Analysis." *Educational Gerontology,* 1990, *16* (1), 27–48.

Kopka, T. L. C., and Peng, S. S. "Adult Education: Main Reasons for Participating. Statistics in Brief." Washington, D.C.: U.S. Department of Education, Office of Educational Research and Improvement, National Center for Education Statistics, 1993.

Kopka, T. L. C., and Peng, S. S. "Statistical Analysis Report: Adult Education: Employment-Related Training." Washington, D.C.: U.S. Department of Education, Office of Educational Research and Improvement, 1994.

Logsdail, K. "The Phenomenon of Learning from Living: A Perspective on Values of Older Adults." Unpublished doctoral dissertation, University of Toronto, 1990.

Lohman, D. F., and Scheurman, G. "Fluid Abilities and Epistemic Thinking: Some Prescriptions for Adult Education." In A. C. Tuijnman and M. Van der Kamp (eds.), *Learning Across the Lifespan: Theories, Research, Policies.* Oxford: Pergamon, 1992.

Lumsden, D. B. *The Older Adult as Learner: Aspects of Educational Gerontology.* Washington, D.C.: Hemisphere, 1985.

Manheimer, R. J., Snodgrass, D. D., and Moskow-McKenzie, D. *Older Adult Education: A Guide to Research, Programs, and Policies.* Westport, Conn.: Greenwood Press, 1995.

Martin, D. M. "Feelings of Loyalty Among Older Adult Students for the Institution of Higher Education Which They Currently Attend as Members of a Learning-in-Retirement Program." Unpublished doctoral dissertation, University of South Carolina, 1995.

Maylor, E. A. "Minimized Prospective Memory Loss in Old Age." In J. Cerella, J. Rybash, W. Hoyer, and M. L. Commons (eds.), *Adult Information Processing: Limits on Loss.* San Diego: Academic Press, 1993.

McDougall, G. J. "Memory Self-Efficacy and Strategy Use in Successful Elders." *Educational Gerontology,* 1995, *21* (4), 357–373.

Merriam, S. B. "The Uses of Reminiscence in Older Adulthood." *Educational Gerontology,* 1993, *19* (5), 441–450.

Michael, R. R. "A Description of Learning in a Group of Well-Elderly over the Age of 75." Unpublished doctoral dissertation, Ball State University, 1991.

Montgomery, R. D. "The Influence of Involvement, Retirement, and Cognitive Age on the Age-Related Learning Deficit." Unpublished doctoral dissertation, Mississippi State University, 1995.

Morris, A. L. "Listening to Older Adult Learners: The Experience Of Using Assistive Technology in Task Performance and Home Modification." Unpublished doctoral dissertation, Virginia Polytechnic Institute and State University, 1995.

O'Connor, D. M. "Motivations of Older College Students: An Analysis of Tuition Waiver Policy for Older Adults in Massachusetts." Unpublished doctoral dissertation, Brandeis University, 1987.

Peterson, D. A. *Facilitating Education for Older Learners.* San Francisco: Jossey-Bass, 1983.

Peterson, D. A., and Wendt, P. F. "Training and Education of Older Americans as Workers and Volunteers." In S. A. Bass (ed.), *Older and Active: How Americans over 55 Are Contributing to Society.* New Haven, Conn.: Yale University, 1995.

Reese, C. G. "The Meaning and Learning of Great-Grandmothering." Unpublished doctoral dissertation, University of Missouri–Saint Louis, 1994.

Rich, G. E. "An Examination of the Processes Older Adults Use to Learn Word Processing Software." Unpublished doctoral dissertation, University of Wisconsin–Madison, 1993.

Salthouse, T. A. "Speed and Knowledge as Determinants of Adult Age Differences in Verbal Tasks." *Journal of Gerontology: Psychological Sciences,* 1993, *48,* P29–P36.

Schacter, D. L., Kihlstrom, J. F., Kaszniak, A. W., and Valdiserri, M. "Preserved and Impaired Memory Functions in Elderly Adults." In J. Cerella, J. Rybash, W. Hoyer, and M. L. Commons (eds.), *Adult Information Processing: Limits on Loss.* San Diego: Academic Press, 1993.

Schaie, K. W. "The Course of Adult Intellectual Development." *American Psychologist,* 1994, *49* (4), 304–313.

Sears, E. J. B. "Self-Directed Learning Projects of Older Adults." Unpublished doctoral dissertation, University of North Texas, 1989.

Sherron, R. M., and Lumsden, D. B. *Introduction to Educational Gerontology* (3rd ed.). New York: Hemisphere, 1990.

Smith, A. D. "Memory." In J. E. Birren and K. W. Schaie (eds.), *Handbook of the Psychology of Aging* (4th ed.). San Diego: Academic Press, 1996.

Stowe, P. "Statistics in Brief. Forty Percent of Adults Participate in Adult Education Activities. Addendum." Washington, D.C.: U.S. Department of Education, Office of Educational Research and Improvement, 1996.

Twitchell, S., Cherry, K. E., and Trott, J. W. "Educational Strategies for Older Learners: Suggestions from Cognitive Aging Research." *Educational Gerontology,* 1996, 22 (2), 169–181.

Walsh, D. A., and Hershey, D. A. "Mental Models and the Maintenance of Complex Problem-Solving Skills in Old Age." In J. Cerella, J. Rybash, W. Hoyer, and M. L. Commons (eds.), *Adult Information Processing: Limits on Loss.* San Diego: Academic Press, 1993.

Willis, S. L. "Introduction to the Special Section on Cognitive Training in Later Adulthood." *Developmental Psychology,* 1990, *26* (6), 875–878.

Wolfe, N. S. "The Relationship Between Successful Aging and Older Adults' Participation in Higher Education Programs." Unpublished doctoral dissertation, University of California, Los Angeles, 1990.

Youngjohn, J. R., and Crook, T. H. "Learning, Forgetting, and Retrieval of Everyday Material Across the Adult Life Span." *Journal of Clinical and Experimental Neuropsychology,* 1993, *15* (4), 447–460.

JAMES C. FISHER is associate professor of adult and continuing education at the University of Wisconsin–Milwaukee.

*A conceptual framework for understanding current practice in the field
of older adult learning is presented. Also discussed are future directions
suggested by current programming that is highly utilized and/or highly
innovative.*

Current Practice and Innovative Programs in Older Adult Learning

Mary-Jane Eisen

The one word that best describes the field of older adult learning is *alternatives*.
At the heart of most long-established programs and new ventures for older learners is the recognition that, although elders are more different from one another
than they are alike, they share a need to be meaningfully connected. Beatty and
Wolf note that "each older adult is unique, possessing a unique story and set of
capacities to meet life's challenges" (1996, pp. 19–20). They also write, "If we are
to connect with older adults, we need to understand how they find meaning and
develop educational approaches to enhance this spirit of individual purpose and
perspective" (p. 26). Clearly no single model will address the diverse interests,
abilities, and access to learning options of all older learners.

The focus of this chapter is threefold: to outline the multilayered context
in which so many learning alternatives have evolved, present an organizing
scheme for this myriad of alternatives, and consider future directions. The
main part of this chapter presents a typology that I have developed to explain
the commonality and diversity among older adult learning programs. To illustrate how the typology is organized, I briefly describe a few well-recognized
older learner programs that boast the highest participation rates. In addition,
an innovative, local program is spotlighted. I conclude by presenting some
principles, gleaned from current practice, that I believe will guide the field of
older adult learning into the next millennium.

What's Been Happening Lately?

When we ask, "What's been happening lately?" we first need to define what
we mean by "lately." The seeds of many current practices were planted over

three decades ago when forecasts of unprecedented demographic shifts gave rise to the 1961 White House Conference on Aging and the resultant passage of the Older Americans and Higher Education Acts in 1965. It was not until the 1970s and 1980s, when federal funding in support of earlier legislation became available, that various educational demonstration projects were launched. These have shaped the landscape of learning options open to elders today. While many successful adult learning models are no longer considered novel, their longevity bears witness to the contribution they have made and continue to make in meeting older learners' needs. A number of service-oriented initiatives that offer opportunities for experiential learning, skill-building, and socialization, such as the Foster Grandparents Program and the Retired Seniors Volunteer Program (RSVP), were in the first wave of program innovations in the 1960s. There is now a renaissance of interest in service-learning among all age groups, along with efforts to cut funding for senior services, especially educational services considered nonessential. Other notable programs with a long history are the college tuition waiver programs, established in the early 1980s, and the ever-expanding educational efforts of senior centers.

Aside from governmental action, certain trends over the past three decades have also elevated the importance of learning in later life. As Cross (1981) points outs, learning was previously relegated to youth, work was the focus of adulthood, and leisure was the reward for reaching old age. In recent years, we have experienced a demographic revolution of unprecedented proportions, along with marked improvements in elders' health and vitality. This has turned the traditional life cycle sequence upside down, calling for a new "blended life cycle" perspective that combines and distributes learning, work, and leisure over the life course.

What Is Happening in the Field of Older Adult Learning?

This chapter provides a way to conceptualize the array of learning options available to older adults. Figure 4.1 presents a four-part typology constructed on two axes that serve as defining elements in describing learning programs for older adults. "For-credit" programs and "noncredit" learning options identify the poles on the vertical axis; "teacher-directed" and "learner-directed" learning are represented on the horizontal axis. The intersection of the two axes creates four quadrants that categorize older adult learning programs and activities. Four other factors—credentialing, convenience, socialization, and personal interests—help to characterize the programs in each of the quadrants.

The Older Adult Learning Typology

The distinction between for-credit and noncredit offerings is generally clear-cut. The middle ground on this axis describes programs that teach specific

Figure 4.1. A Typology of Older Adult Learning Programs

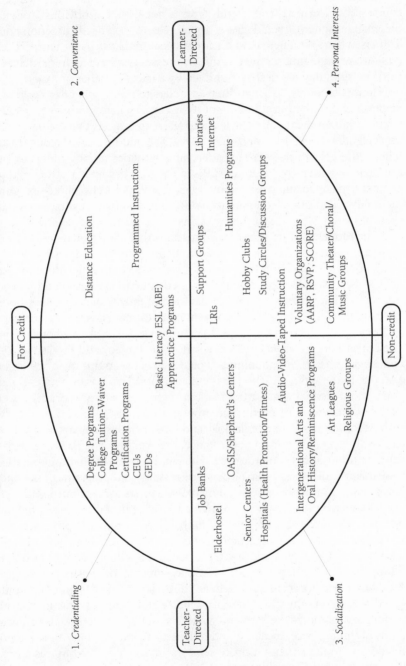

skills or concepts, but may not be authorized to grant generally accepted "credits," as do colleges. On the other hand, what distinguishes teacher-directed courses from learner-directed endeavors is not always as obvious. For example, many teacher-directed classes today seek to foster self-direction among learners and are designed around learners' goals rather than the teacher's interests. At the same time, some self-directed learners may elect to participate in certain classes that are designed and led by a master teacher or expert.

In this typology, "teacher-directed" refers to traditional offerings that are planned by expert-educators for groups of learners. Learner-directed generally refers to more individualized, self-paced learning projects that are designed or implemented by older learners themselves. The middle ground along this axis reflects the growth in peer-based learning activities among older learners. Learning in Retirement Institutes (LRIs) are a good example of structured programming planned and executed by peers. Study circles and discussion groups exemplify the informal counterpart of LRIs; unlike LRIs, they have existed for centuries.

The top left quadrant contains programs that are for credit and teacher-centered. This includes college degree programs, professional designation programs, General Education Diplomas (GEDs), and continuing education units (CEUs). As just indicated, teacher-centered courses are designed by expert-teachers with a view to meeting explicit requirements of accrediting bodies. They are usually delivered in a conventional, formal classroom setting, with set meeting times and assignments, to groups of learners, all of whom are interested in earning a *credential* of some sort. Basic literacy and English as a second language (ESL) programming is placed in between this quadrant and the next one to the right, close to the horizontal axis. This positioning in the diagram acknowledges that participants in such programs are seeking specific skills and may want or need some proof of their mastery, but the delivery of such education may be more flexible, and formal credits may not be given. Literacy Volunteers of America, for instance, uses volunteers who are not expert-teachers to do one-to-one tutoring. The emphasis in the first quadrant is on credentialing for professional or personal reasons, and programs in that quadrant would most likely be selected by older learners for that purpose.

Others may also be interested in credentials, but if they place a premium on personal *convenience,* they would probably be attracted to programs in the top right quadrant, where distance education is located. Distance education, usually offered by higher education providers, is a self-guided approach to fulfilling the requirements of an accredited degree or certificate program. Although there is considerable teacher direction in the design of computer-based training modules and supplementary study guides, this increasingly popular option offers the learner a good deal of freedom to exercise choice in terms of timing, pace, location, and independent exploration of the material. In addition to universities, private vendors are forging ahead in this arena as the availability of affordable, user-friendly, personal computers and videotape players proliferates. Access issues related to physical disability, rural geographic location, or lack of safe transportation make this option especially appealing to some older learners.

Also in the second quadrant, but closer to the center, are programmed instruction and a low-tech alternative, the apprentice program. Both teach specific skills on an individualized basis, and, although they may not grant credit per se, they often fulfill employability requirements. Self-paced programmed instruction is frequently provided through corporate training centers. Apprenticeships, which involve on-the-job work experience under a skilled person's tutelage, are usually sponsored by trade unions. As more older persons choose to keep working or find that they cannot afford to retire, the need for job training, retraining, and preparation for second or third careers is growing. In summary, this quadrant, like the first one, represents those learning alternatives that grant credit or meet some specified requirements. The choices here, however, are more oriented to the learner's needs for convenience in terms of access and individualization.

Programs in the bottom left quadrant, such as those offered by senior centers, Elderhostel, hospitals, or intergenerational education programs, serve the largest numbers of older learners today. These programs are almost always elective in nature, they are teacher-centered (those closer to the middle are more peer-based), and they range from educational to creative to informational. They are popular among large numbers of older adults who do not want the pressure associated with for-credit courses but who like the structure of an organized delivery system. Some value the expert-teacher as a source of knowledge, others enjoy the group learning setting, and others look forward to a predictable routine that will fill their leisure time in a meaningful way. The diversity in older learner preferences indicates variation in the definition of what is meaningful. Intellectual stimulation is usually part of it, but many offerings in this quadrant are attractive because of their other features, such as travel, health promotion, or recreation. The one common denominator of the programs in this quadrant, then, is *socialization*.

Personal interests are probably the strongest attraction for older learners who select activities or resources from the bottom right quadrant, such as libraries, the Internet, hobby clubs, support groups, and study circles. This last section of the typology contains noncredit activities that are directed either by the learner and his or her peers, or by the learner alone. Although these learning projects may be less formal, they may be very intensive, depending on the individual elder.

Significantly, shifts occur as we move from left to right on the horizontal axis. The teacher-directed programs have more of an educational or informational content delivery focus, whereas the peer-based alternatives place greater emphasis on social interaction in conjunction with intellectual stimulation. The learner-directed efforts tend to center on very specific learner interests. These might involve short-term information-seeking efforts to address an immediate need, or the practice of a lifelong hobby or passion now that more time is available for such pursuits. At the same time, there is movement from a more formal learning design to a more experiential, self-directed approach, sometimes alone, sometimes in the company of others.

Generally, there will be a quadrant of best fit for any given older learning program or activity, but some, because of their unique philosophy or design, may float among two or more quadrants. Likewise, some educational providers may specialize in one type of learning, while others may offer several types. Depending on their primary needs and preferences at a given time, older learners may be inclined to choose programs that fall within one particular quadrant. However, it is possible for older learners to be engaged in activities from all four quadrants at once. Of course, as individuals' needs change over time, their preferences are likely to shift too. Fisher's (1993) study of seventy-four elders between the ages of 61 and 94 resulted in a framework for developmental change that suggests increasing needs for socialization throughout the older years, and for individualized or peer-based support at two key transition points in older adulthood.

Where Is Older Adult Learning Happening?

Higher education institutions, local adult education services (run by cities, towns, or community-based organizations), and employers are the major providers of for-credit, teacher-directed programming described in the first quadrant. In some cases, where legislation has required certain types of training, private training consultants and nonprofit educational organizations have also moved into this arena. Tuition waiver programs, available in most states, have done a lot to encourage participation by older learners in college coursework. On the noncredit side of Figure 4.1, there are many more alternatives. Those in the third quadrant are more formal, those in the middle are more peer oriented, and those on the right are the most self-directed. The highest utilization in the noncredit quadrants is found in educational programming at senior centers, which have been expanding in an effort to attract new, younger retirees, at Elderhostel, and at Shepherd's Centers and OASIS programs around the nation. In the middle are various employer-sponsored training activities, including technological skill building. What follows are brief overviews of these types of programs, selected for further discussion because of their broad-based utilization and corresponding impact.

Workplace, Vocational, and Technological Education. The majority of training and development dollars spent in the United States today are expended by business and industry. More older learners are becoming the beneficiaries of corporate training efforts as the number of new entrants into the job market declines, a result of the "baby bust" of the 1970s. In addition, younger cohorts of elders are finding that they have a financial need to continue working or a desire to remain engaged productively in light of longer life expectancy. There is also evidence that workplaces of the future will move even more in the direction of flexible working schedules, telecommuting, and project-based work arrangements, all of which will enable older adults to contribute on a flexible part-time, seasonal, or temporary basis. At the same time, through their tuition reimbursement plans, corporations are among the biggest supporters of for-credit higher education and professional certification programs. Some even offer on-site degree program courses.

Younger cohorts of seniors are increasingly computer literate and increasingly cognizant of the demand for lifelong learning in connection with technology and other advances. Although training for technological proficiency is nowhere more urgent than in business and industry, the use of technology has become so popular that it is being used by many older persons for non-work-related pursuits, such as socializing and self-directed learning projects.

The American Association of Retired Persons (AARP) publications "How to Train Older Workers" (1993) and "American Business and Older Workers: A Roadmap to the 21st Century" (1995), and AARP's National Older Workers Information System (NOWIS) are recommended as resources for more information on this topic.

Higher Education. Taking college courses on a tuition-waiver, space-available basis is one of the most popular forms of continuing education for seniors. Yet the majority of older college students prefer the audit option, seeking learning primarily for learning's sake, rather than in pursuit of a degree. According to Sylvia Gordon (personal communication, West Hartford, Connecticut, September 16, 1997), president of the Senior Renewal Club at Capitol Community-Technical College in Hartford, Connecticut, there are over two hundred members, ranging in age from 62 up to their late 80s, who take courses regularly and belong to the Club. Usually, however, only one student earns a degree each year. Others just keep going, sometimes repeating classes, "for the sheer joy of being there." For many, going to college was not possible during the Great Depression, and now is the time to fulfill an old dream. The opportunity to take classes with students of all ages and to belong to a club, such as the Senior Renewal Club, clearly adds a social dimension to the collegiate experience. The Senior Renewal Club has added another element, too. Its members have decided to give something back to the college by funding twelve scholarships and some special equipment purchases each year.

On the other hand, Barbara Ginsberg (telephone interview, Brooklyn, New York, September 6,1997), director of the My Turn Program at Kingsborough Community College in Brooklyn, New York, expects the trickle of graduating elders to turn into a flood in the years to come. Barbara Guttmann-Gee is one such older learner who reports that she derived "a long-awaited sense of well-being, enhanced self-worth and power" from earning a bachelor's degree at age 75 and a master's degree at age 81 (1995–1996, p. 1). A proponent of for-credit education, Ginsberg was instrumental in recently starting an organization of and for senior learners, City University Options for Older Learners (COOL). With eighteen branches and only twenty members so far, one of COOL's goals is to restore tuition waivers for the four-year City University degree programs comparable to what the community colleges have been offering continuously since 1976.

If future cohorts of older persons elect to continue their professional employment, make career changes later in life, or alter their perceptions of socially constructed roles for elders, more of them may choose to pursue formal degrees after age 60. Other factors that might lead to increased interest in degree programs include younger cohorts' anticipation of extended life expectancy and improved health, the need for a continuous income, and employers' increasing willingness to retain and retrain older workers. The fact that younger cohorts of seniors are better educated also bodes well for formal, degree programs because prior educational achievement has been shown to be the single best indicator of later participation in educational pursuits (Manheimer, Snodgrass, and Moskow-McKenzie, 1995).

In addition, the rapidly accelerating use of personal computers has opened new frontiers in distance education, offering highly accessible, flexible, self-paced options for people of all ages to complete degree programs. (For a fuller discussion of distance learning, please see Chapter Six of this volume.)

Many more adult learning offerings fall on the noncredit side of the continuum. In fact, given the explosion of people over age 60, relatively few take advantage of the tuition waiver programs at community colleges around the country. "The reasons for lack of enrollment include the fact that many people do not know about the program, others lack transportation. . . . But probably the most important reason is that older adults simply do not want the kind of learning offered by conventional higher education" (Moody in Manheimer, Snodgrass, Moskow-McKenzie, 1995, p. 142). Options outside of the higher education arena are plentiful, and often they are more attractive to elders because they are less structured and have a secondary focus, such as socialization, recreation, travel, or community service.

Elderhostel. Perhaps the most well-known older adult learning program is Elderhostel. Started in 1974 as a small-scale, inexpensive learn-and-travel opportunity in the northeast, this popular model has since gone international, offering classes of one or more weeks in duration throughout the year. Recent innovations include special grandparent-grandchild weeks and adventure programs for the young-old. Although Elderhostel classes are typically teacher directed, flexibility is central to this model. Elderhostelers are expected to attend all classes, but they are free to be serious or casual students. For some, the travel component and the extracurricular activities or the opportunity to combine the Elderhostel experience with a family reunion may take precedence over the courses.

OASIS and the Shepherd's Centers. The Older Adult Service and Information System (OASIS) and the Shepherd's Centers are two other well-established educational models that offer regularly scheduled noncredit courses at very minimal cost to participants. Each has centers in several American cities and serves upward of one hundred thousand elders per year. OASIS is sponsored nationally by the May Department Stores Company, and the Shepherd's Centers are sponsored by local coalitions of religious congregations. While many of their courses are taught by outside teachers, both programs encourage peer teaching and participant involvement in planning and community service activities.

Learning in Retirement Institutes. Learning in Retirement Institutes (LRIs) are nonprofit membership organizations, numbering over two hundred nationally. They are generally affiliated with an institution of higher education that provides classroom facilities and some administrative support. By and large, however, LRIs are run by members for members. Since their noncredit courses are taught by retirees who are experts in their fields, the range of courses depends on the availability of seniors who wish to teach their peers. The first institute of this type began in the early 1960s at the New School for Social Research in New York City, but the concept gained widespread acceptance in the 1980s, with the most significant growth since 1989.

An exemplary LRI is the College for Seniors at the University of North Carolina at Asheville (UNCA). Operating in cooperation with two related initiatives on the same campus, Leadership Asheville Seniors and The Senior Academy for Intergenerational Learning (all programs of the North Carolina Center for Creative Retirement), this active LRI offers continuous learning through study and fellowship, community service, and intergenerational cooperation. By forging opportunities for productive engagement, both the community and the older residents benefit.

Intergenerational Programs. Ranging from simple school- or community-based tutoring arrangements to reciprocal caregiving initiatives, oral history programming, joint choirs, and collaborative arts projects, the field of intergenerational learning is blooming. Some elders seek regular contact with other generations, while others are inspired to solve social or civic problems through community service. In some cases, a mutual love of theater or art can connect people of different generations.

Three specific innovative models illustrate the diversity in this one area of older adult learning. First, the ten-year-old Senior Academy for Intergenerational Learning (SAIL) connects senior volunteers with the University of North Carolina at Asheville by having them serve as mentors to students and as consultants to faculty and staff.

Since 1979, EldersShareTheArts, Inc. (ESTA), of New York City has endeavored to validate elders' life experience and create community through the arts (Perlstein, 1991). Bringing generations and cultures together through creative arts and humanities programs is their forte. Their centerpiece program is the Living History Theatre workshop that runs for thirty weeks at community centers, senior centers, and schools in the metropolitan area, culminating in multigenerational performances or art exhibitions. Like many organizations that survive on an assortment of government grants, private donations, and nominal fees for service, this organization has to be resourceful. It recently economized by sharing space with CityLore, an urban folklore advocacy. Their use of shared space reflects common values and commitments with respect to heritage and community building.

The Intergenerational Urban Institute at Worcester State College in Worcester, Massachusetts, was established in 1995 to "harness the combined talents of college students of all ages to meet the . . . challenges that face our urban environment" (1996). Because Worcester State College is affiliated with a consortium of local higher education institutions, it can draw on a variety of traditional, nontraditional, and elder students. Debates and forums on intergenerational issues, pre-retirement planning programs, and outreach efforts, as well as an intergenerational arts collaborative, have helped to build a multigenerational learning community. Several ongoing volunteer programs have developed a service community as well. Beneficiaries of these efforts come from many age groups, including teenage parents, older homeowners in financial crisis, and foreign college students.

Senior Centers.   Identified by the federal Administration on Aging, U.S. Department of Health and Human Services, as "focal points," senior centers are indeed a clearinghouse for many elders across the country. They serve as a primary point of access into the aging network within any given community, usually offering essential services such as health screenings and hot meals as well as basic information and referral services. Because of their geographic and financial accessibility, they are probably the most widely used educational resource for elders.

Frequently, senior centers are co-located with Area Agencies on Aging, Councils on Aging, and other organizing bodies that coordinate community services and resources for older adults age 60 and older. However, as the population of people age 85 and older grows, these centers find themselves catering to the frailer "old-old" population and becoming less attractive to newly retired, more active "young-old" cohorts (Neugarten, 1996). Accordingly, senior centers are being forced to stretch. "Many have abandoned their social-club beginnings to provide services like support groups for grandparents raising grandchildren, lectures on crime prevention and computer classes" (Stock, 1996, p. C-1).

As the number of elders grows, the size of special interest groups increases, creating a demand for special programming, such as immigrants in need of ESL classes and physically challenged populations in need of classes that offer special accommodations. Simultaneously, spending cuts place limits on already overextended senior centers and mitigate against institutionalizing the frailest elders. Thus the centers are left to meet increasingly diverse needs related to members' health status, coping strategies, basic skills, and recreational desires. As a result, most senior centers emphasize instrumental learning and basic recreational programming. In their efforts to serve large numbers of diverse elders, the danger is that many provide what I would call holding spaces rather than learning spaces. This is not to say that they do not offer caring communities to their members. Indeed, for many elders, their senior center is their surrogate family. Nevertheless, according to Manheimer, Snodgrass, and Moskow-McKenzie (1995, p. 88), "No list exists of senior centers that offer intellectually challenging programming or that might involve members in important leadership roles."

Nevertheless, senior centers do serve an important maintenance function in the lives of elders by offering a broad range of program offerings and by focusing on the immediate instrumental learning needs of their members.

What Is Happening That Is Really Exciting?

The most exciting older adult learning alternatives focus on the ongoing developmental needs of their participants. The LRI model and the three intergenerational learning programs mentioned previously fit into this category. One other exemplary initiative is the Hartford Artisans' Center in Hartford, Connecticut.

The Hartford Artisans' Center is the fortunate outcome of the resourceful partnering of two visionaries dedicated to helping elders and people with disabilities lead fuller lives: Edjohnetta Miller, artist and teacher, and Rebecca Earl, vice president for Program and Staff Development at the Connecticut Institute for the Blind. By working together, they merged their separate visions into one very powerful mission: bringing men and women with disabilities and people over age 55 together to create beautiful things that are sold for a profit. Community development block grants through the City of Hartford Elderly Services Division, funds from private foundations and givers, as well as support from the Connecticut Institute for the Blind allowed the center to open on December 5, 1995. Now as many as thirty-five students pay dues of five dollars per month to learn how to make finely crafted fiber arts, become proficient enough to produce high-quality products for sale, and participate in strategic business planning for the center's future. There is no formal recruitment of learners. Word of mouth keeps the center filled.

Miller's teaching practice reflects her firm belief that each person possesses an inner artist. This philosophy is very powerful in itself, but the production component of the plan really makes it sizzle. It gives the artisans monetary and psychological recognition and, eventually, it will enable the center to become self-sustaining.

The center helps people reclaim their self-worth, or develop it anew, through serious artwork, skill building, and accountability for producing something that has aesthetic as well as market value. When goods are sold, the center and the artisans share in the proceeds—both the monetary returns and the accolades. Orders keep coming in from around the country, and the artisans keep filling them, attesting to the success of this unique formula.

Integration is a powerful theme at the Hartford Artisans' Center. This refers not only to integrating people of different backgrounds, races, and abilities in order to build a community of artists but also to integrating artistry into daily life as well. Also evident is a keen awareness of the profoundly human need to integrate socialization, creativity, and productivity in our daily work and play. In addition, there is an integration of carefully practiced craftsmanship and skill with the improvisational artistry and serendipity of quilting, and, finally, the personal integration that comes with "finding oneself through art," as Miller puts it (personal communication, Hartford, Connecticut, June 23, 1997).

Erik Erikson's (1963) renowned eight-stage model of human development culminates with the struggle between integration and despair. At the Hartford Artisans' Center, many participants have found a way to overcome the despair of infirmities or physical limitations. They have accomplished this by forming bonds at the center with the teachers and co-learners, much as the infant in Erikson's first stage forms an attachment in order to derive the virtue of hope (1963). Participants have a sense of will and purpose fostered by opportunities at the center to exercise autonomy and initiative in their craft. Certainly, they develop feelings of competence as they move from amateur status to artisan, and this competency is a source of their evolving identity as contributive human beings. The caring spirit that permeates the center is an antidote to the isolation that many struggle with in later adulthood. The productive component of the program emphasizes the defining role of generativity at every stage. With all these components in place, it is no wonder that the culminating virtue of integration is so much in evidence.

Concluding Remarks

The future of older adult learning will surely carry forth the emphasis on alternatives that characterizes current practice. After all, the "me" generation will begin to turn 60 in a few years. This generation can be expected to demand even more options and will want them faster and at the best price. In addition to options, I have gleaned at least three principles from what I consider to be among the best of today's practices: the North Carolina Center for Creative Retirement, ESTA, the Intergenerational Urban Institute at Worcester State College, and the Hartford Artisans' Center. I urge planners of older adult learning to build the following three principles into their offerings to ensure the highest-quality programming for older persons:

- Learning communities blossom when they are tended with care and fertilized by diversity. Connecting people to people in a caring way is powerful in itself, but bringing together people of different ages, abilities, backgrounds, and cultures has the potential to take learning to a higher level.
- Creative partnering (of visionary people and organizations) will produce new combinations and ever-exciting alternatives. It will also ensure survival in a field that continues to be underfunded.
- Paying tribute to the contributive nature of human beings brings out the best in learners. It is essential to honor learners' humanity (their unique gifts), heritage (their grounding), and creative spirit (their potential) by providing a safe space for people to try out new things and question taken-for-granted assumptions about their own limits.

Much as the artisan quilters at the Hartford Artisans' Center piece together bits of fabric to compose a work of art that touches its viewers, this chapter brings together the many components of older adult learning to aid in understanding this growing field and fuel commitment to its continuing evolution.

References

American Association of Retired Persons. "American Business and Older Workers: A Road Map to the 21st Century." Washington, D.C., 1995.

American Association of Retired Persons. "How to Train Older Workers." Washington, D.C., 1993.

Beatty, P. T., and Wolf, M. A. *Connecting with Older Adults: Educational Responses and Approaches.* Malabar, Fla.: Kreiger, 1996.

Cross, K. P. *Adults as Learners: Increasing Participation and Facilitating Learning.* San Francisco: Jossey-Bass, 1981.

Erikson, E. H. *Childhood and Society* (2nd ed.). New York: W. W. Norton, 1963.

Fisher, J. C. "A Framework for Describing Developmental Change Among Older Adults." *Adult Education Quarterly,* 1993, *43* (2), 76–89.

Guttmann-Gee, B. "The Power of Education for the Older Learner." *The Older Learner,* 1995–1996, *4* (1), 1–8.

Intergenerational Urban Institute. Mission statement. Worcester, Mass.: Worcester State College, 1996.

Manheimer, R. J., Snodgrass, D. D., and Moskow-McKenzie, D. *Older Adult Education: A Guide to Research, Programs and Policies.* Asheville, N.C.: Greenwood Press, 1995.

Neugarten, B. L. *The Meanings of Age.* Chicago: University of Chicago Press, 1996.

Perlstein, S. "Elders Share the Arts." *Generations,* Spring 1991.

Stock, R. W. "Centers for Elderly Enter a New Age." *New York Times,* Dec. 26, 1996, C1–C8.

MARY-JANE EISEN is a doctoral candidate in the AEGIS program at Teachers College at Columbia University and teaches human development at the University of Hartford and Saint Joseph College in West Hartford, Connecticut.

*Policy for older adult education is considerably limited, but sorely
needed. This lack of policy has held back the development of the field,
reduced its impact, and allowed the development of a diverse and
uncoordinated set of instructional programs. Leadership is needed in
order to reverse this situation.*

Policy for Older Adult Education

David A. Peterson, Hiromi Masunaga

For centuries, humans have been defined as social animals, guided in their
relationships by policies set forth in law. An example of this phenomenon is
the initiation of public education and the drastic changes it caused in family
interactions. Public schooling took over an important role of adults in the family—the provision of information and socialization of offspring. Not only have
policy decisions influenced social interactions, but policies themselves have
also been shaped by changing demands within a society. For instance, current
demographic changes in the United States have resulted in renewed consideration of medical care and financial security of the older adult population.

This chapter concerns policy decisions in the area of older adult education. Specifically, the following two questions are addressed in this chapter: (1)
Why have so few policies on older adult education guided learning-related
interactions among humans? (2) What policy decisions are needed for the
future, in order to enhance practices of older adult education?

Current Participation of Older Adults in Education

The older adult population has become more and more visible, mainly because
of its increasing size and proportion of the population. Longer life expectancy
and longer life after retirement have encouraged older adults to participate in
various emerging and expanding activities, especially those that involve new
experiences, contributions to society, and learning. For instance, the Elderhostel program, a residential educational program for anyone over the age of
55, was initiated in 1974 and has rapidly grown to enroll over 300,000 older
adult participants annually. Currently it offers instruction in more than 1,999
facilities, such as universities and colleges, in more than forty countries around
the world (Mills, 1993).

The growth of the Elderhostel program leads to the perception that a large number of older adults are currently participating in educational programs. However, this perception does not reflect reality. It is widely recognized that 4 to 6 percent of senior adults participate in organized educational programs annually (Lowy and O'Connor, 1986). This is a very small percentage of a population that has the time and resources to participate. Although a precise definition of educational participation is difficult, it is clear that most older people do not attend courses that meet for several sessions.

Moody (1976) presented a four-stage model of education for the older adult: (1) rejection, (2) social services, (3) participation, and (4) self-actualization. The first stage, rejection, reflects the isolation of the aged in modern societies, in which "old people are, functionally speaking, nonentities" (Moody, 1976, p. 3). The second stage, social services, defines older adult education as leisure-time activities. The third stage, participation, prepares older adults for new roles in society through breaking stereotypes of old age. The fourth stage, self-actualization, focuses on the potential of older people to psychologically grow through learning. Moody concluded that the most current educational programs were directed at stages three and four, encouraging educators to respond to the needs of the least needy aged. Twenty years have passed since he described his hopes for future practice, but it is clear that these programs still are not widely available.

The strong need for progress in older adult education was also described as early as the 1950s by Donahue (1955), and few real innovations have occurred since that time. In his recent work, Moody contends that "the most important observation about education for older adults in America is that the enterprise is not serious. Unless we get serious about late-life learning, we will fail to adopt appropriate means to promote productive aging in the years to come. The lack of seriousness in older-adult education is shown by almost any measure we adopt: numbers of students enrolled, money and other resources committed to the enterprise, level of sophistication in the delivery systems deployed" (1993, p. 221).

Why Policies on Education for Older People Are Limited

Although educational gerontology is often described as a single program, it is best viewed as being comprised of three aspects: older adult education, education about aging, and education of professionals who will work with and on behalf of older persons. The emphasis here is on the first area and how it can be influenced by national and state policy. Existing policies for older adult education are examined here to identify strengths and weaknesses in the current policy decisions that regulate educational opportunities for adults who are at least 55 years old.

The most impressive characteristic of policy as it relates to older adult education is that there is so little of it and that it has had such limited impact.

Policy options can be placed in one of two categories—those that are intended to influence society, and those that are intended to influence individuals. There has never been sufficient pressure from older people, educators, elected officials, or agency staff to design, support, and implement policy for this area. Older adult education could be effective in such areas as increasing the level of literacy, preparing immigrants for citizenship, helping persons prepare financially for retirement, facilitating second careers, and encouraging the maintenance of independence. For instance, policies on older adult education in preparation for retirement can focus on both the individual and society. Financial and psychological well-being of an older adult after retirement is not only of great concern for the particular individual but also quite influential to, say, the financial and economic well-being of the society. A huge asset to the U.S. economy would be a workforce of older adults at retirement age who are well adjusted to new technological demands through educational programs aimed at preparing them for a second career.

One reason for the lack of policy initiatives is that education for persons of all ages is the responsibility of the state, not the federal, government. Groups of older people have tended to direct their political activity at the national, rather than the state, level. Organizations such as the American Association of Retired Persons (AARP) and the National Council on the Aging (NCOA) have primarily carried their requests to Congress and the President, while few organizations stressed attempts to achieve change through state government. Among the few examples of state policy are seniors in connection with the University of Massachusetts–Boston who have been active and successful in getting state legislation passed, and the Silver Haired Legislatures, who have also been active in several states.

Policies on Education for Older People—Existing Policies and Policies in Need

Government policies that concern individuals might emphasize helping older adults know the options that exist, assisting them in planing for future goal achievement, and helping them make wise decisions about their own lives. Educational practices guided by these policies help older adults set goals and achieve them. For some people, the goal is to learn about opportunities to travel, to find volunteer roles, to become familiar with new technologies, to share their life stories with others, to complete a degree, or to understand their own aging. Additional goals for the frail older person include being able to afford to stay in one's own home, obtaining appropriate care regardless of ability to pay, understanding the ethical options available to the oldest old, and exercising the right to be helped by professionals who are knowledgeable about aging and older people. Thus, the emphasis is on older adults achieving their own goals. In order to effectively attain the goal of helping a person, government support needs to be available to encourage well-organized educational programs.

Several areas of policy opportunities exist in older adult education. Policies are needed that will encourage the involvement of middle-aged and older adults in lifelong learning. While a few major programs such as Institutes for Lifetime Learning and Elderhostel report large enrollments, the rate of actual participation among the entire older adult population is extremely limited. In 1976, the Lifelong Learning Act, which encouraged the broadening of educational activities for older persons, was passed by Congress. Since it was never funded, implementation was very modest and resulted in little additional action or leadership from the federal government. One approach that has been used by several states is to offer free or greatly reduced tuition to older persons who wish to enroll in college classes on a space-available basis (Timmermann, 1981). A public college or university in many states can allow older learners to sit in on classes when there is room, but the institution does not receive any state aid for teaching these students as they do for matriculated students, so there is little incentive to make the opportunity widely known or to recruit participants. Thus, the first policy approach is to encourage participation in educational programs by older people.

A second needed policy is one that will broaden the diversity of participants. Only a small minority of older people participate in organized classes. While many more undertake independent learning projects (Hiemstra, 1975; Tough, 1971) most older people, especially minority individuals and those with limited formal education, do not enroll in any learning experiences. Policy is needed that encourages participation by giving tax incentives, enhancing social security or Medicare benefits, or advertising the potential values of such participation.

Manheimer, Snodgrass, and Moskow-McKenzie pointed out the lack of a single dominant model of older adult education: "Different groups have a stake in older adult education and related policies but view older adults and their education differently. For example, some educational organizations claim or accept responsibility for education which targets a certain group of citizens, older adults being one of them. Aging organizations, on the other hand, claim or accept responsibility for older adult programs that happen to be educational" (1995, p. 121). This suggests that noncentralized educational practices make it difficult for older adults to acquire sufficient information on and participate in educational practices.

Thus, a third policy could encourage the development of special organizations that offer education for older people as a primary or exclusive task and as the single focus of the educational institution. A wide variety of organizations currently offer instructional programs resulting in diversity of quality, purpose, and method. These organizations should not be mirror images of each other, but rather should have specific emphases within a generally accepted framework. For instance, some would emphasize service to minority participants, some would prepare participants for second careers, and all should have low fees and high quality. (The assumption is made here that people would rather participate with others of similar ethnic, religious, or economic backgrounds.) Also, for all programs, essential information such as curriculum, purpose, cost, time, and location should be readily available to future participants from a single source.

Current programs for older people are offered in community organizations, educational institutions, senior centers, nursing homes, and churches, to name a few. In each case, education for older people is just an add-on, often seen as being outside the mission of the institution. What is needed is an organization that has education for older people as its primary interest and therefore can give leadership to the field. The actual trend, however, is for instructional programs to be increasingly offered by profit-making organizations. These programs provide instruction on health, investments, second careers, and so on, and they emphasize any topic that can be sold at a profit. Some of these programs are of good quality, but occasionally they are scams to separate older people from their money. Although continuing education by institutions of higher education is common, it has not been integrated into the credit programs and often functions as a second-class add-on to the regular academic offerings of the institution. Therefore, as private corporations find topics on which they can turn a profit, they compete with traditional providers. This is seen in instruction offered by investment firms, hospitals, nursing homes, banks, health care organizations, and computer companies.

The diversity of institutions, organizations, and businesses that offer instructional programs makes it difficult to measure their quality and outcomes. This need for guidance in evaluating educational programs is the fourth proposed policy. Because learning is voluntary, evaluation of learning is frequently replaced by a satisfaction index that shows the participants' response but does not measure whether any learning occurred. It is up to the local program staff to carry out the evaluations. The staff frequently does not have the resources or the expertise to do so, relegating the assessment of impact to an occasional or nonexistent activity.

A fifth policy issue deals with the preparation and expertise of the instructors. Today, practically anyone can teach older adults. No preparation is required, no credential is needed, and no evaluation is completed. Thus, the quality of these programs is quite variable. The participant has no way of knowing what the level of instruction is or whether the teacher has expertise, skill, and experience. Policy is needed that will ensure quality by setting some standards for initial credentialing and subsequent regular assurance of continued skill and knowledge.

Faculty preparation and quality of the programs in which faculty are trained are also important. Since there is no accreditation of gerontology instruction, it is impossible to know which schools have good programs and which have unacceptable ones in preparing good potential faculty in older adult education. Policy development on college program accreditation, such as the Association for Gerontology and Higher Education (AGHE) Standards and Guidelines, the materials from the Consultation Project, and the many other reports that have been completed over the past several years, should be further facilitated.

A sixth policy issue is who should pay for older adult instruction—the learner, the federal government, or the state. In general, for instruction to be funded, a policy would need to be developed at the state or federal level that would show the level of commitment by the government and the standard on the impact on the students. Support from the federal government would allow it to set priorities for content to be emphasized. It could, as was done in the state of California, reimburse providers for expenses involved in offering "survival education"—that which would help older people maintain their independence.

A seventh policy issue is durability of the program. Since many educational programs for older people are offered as a supplement to the primary work of the organization, the programs can be canceled or dismantled just as quickly as they can be created. Thus, policy spelling out the long-term commitments to the program is necessary and helpful to the older person seeking instruction.

Policy for older adult education is considerably limited, but sorely needed. The lack of policy has held back the development of the field, reduced its impact, and allowed the development of a diverse and uncoordinated set of instructional programs. Leadership is needed in order to reverse this situation, but none is visible yet. In this rapidly aging society, the need exists for educational innovations delineated by Moody twenty years ago—serious older adult educational programs with a focus on the third and fourth stages, that is, participation of older adults in society and older adults' self-actualization. Productive aging of an individual reflects productive functioning of the society, and vice versa.

References

Donahue, W. *Education for Later Maturity: A Handbook.* New York: Whiteside, 1955.

Hiemstra, R.P. *The Older Adult and Learning.* Lincoln, Neb.: University of Nebraska, 1975.

Lowy, L., and O'Connor, D. *Why Education in the Later Years?* Lexington, Mass.: Lexington Books, 1986.

Manheimer, R. L., Snodgrass, D. D., and Moskow-McKenzie, D. M. *Older Adult Education.* London: Greenwood Press, 1995.

Mills, E. S. *The Story of Elderhostel.* Hanover, N. H.: University Press of New England, 1993.

Moody, H. R. "Philosophical Presuppositions of Education for Old Age." *Educational Gerontology.* 1976, *1* (1), 1–16.

Moody, H. R. "A Strategy for Productive Aging: Education in Later Life." In S. A. Bass, G. Caro, and Y. P.Chen (eds.), *Achieving a Productive Aging Society.* Westport, Conn.: Auburn House, 1993.

Timmermann, S. "Education for Older Persons in the U.S.A." Paper presented at the 12th International Congress of Gerontology, Hamburg, Germany, July 1981.

Tough, A. *The Adult's Learning Projects.* Austin, Tex.: Learning Concepts, 1971.

DAVID A. PETERSON is professor and director of Leonard Davis School of Gerontology, Ethel Percy Andrus Gerontology Center, University of Southern California, Los Angeles.

HIROMI MASUNAGA is a research associate at the University of Southern California.

This chapter addresses what we already know about older learners and information technology, describes some exemplary programs, discusses the potential and the limitations of using computer technology for older adult learning, and considers future trends.

The Role of Information Technology in Older Adult Learning

Sandra Timmermann

Two trends are converging as we reach the year 2000: the increase in the number of older people and the growth of the information technology industry. Understanding how older learners can take advantage of the technological revolution for learning, and providing them with access to computers, the Internet, and other technologies will be one of the greatest challenges and opportunities for older adult educators in the next few years.

Profile of Older Computer Users

It is difficult to keep up with statistics on the use of computers and the Internet by older adults because information technology is moving so rapidly, and more and more people of all ages find themselves on the information highway. Findings from a study conducted by Adler (1996) on computer ownership among adults age 55 to 74 indicate that 30 percent own a computer. This was a dramatic increase from a study completed just eighteen months earlier by the same organization that found that 21 percent of people in this age group owned a computer (Adler, 1996). Based on these figures, one can easily predict that computer usage will continue to expand considerably for older adults.

What is perhaps more significant is the number of older Internet users. Several studies indicate that 14 percent of Internet users are over age 50 (Katz, 1997, Third Age Media and the Excite Network, 1997). The increases in Internet usage in just a year or two are dramatic. Internet usage by people of all ages is increasing by 10 percent per month (Negroponte, 1996, p. 6). It is very likely that this trend will continue as computer technology becomes more accessible and less costly.

NEW DIRECTIONS FOR ADULT AND CONTINUING EDUCATION, no. 77, Spring 1998 © Jossey-Bass Publishers

The characteristics of those older adults who own computers or are online may not be surprising to adult educators. Paralleling the statistics of the characteristics of older people who participate in adult education programs, computer ownership and online participation rise significantly with the level of formal education and socioeconomic status. According to Third Age Media and the Excite Network (1997), 50 percent of people over age 50 who use the Internet have college degrees or higher and nearly one-third earn more than $70,000 per year. The one difference between older computer users and older adults who participate in adult education programs, however, is the greater proportion of male online users.

Early Adopters. One might speculate that older adults who decide to purchase a computer and learn how to use it are the "early adopters." They are likely to be self-directed lifelong learners—individuals with the motivation and curiosity to follow their own learning project, in this case, how to use computers and computer technology. Third Age Media and the Excite Network (1997) found that adults over the age of 50 are motivated by a desire to "try something new," more so than younger users. "Trying something new" was cited by 67 percent in response to the question, "Why did you go online in the first place?"

Making intergenerational connections is also a strong motivational factor in why older adults use computers and go online. Many older adults purchase computers to communicate by e-mail with their adult children and grandchildren. Some, in fact, are urged by their family members to buy a computer and go online. Many older adults, particularly those who live more than 50 miles from their families, are willing to try out electronic communication because they are not able to get together face to face as frequently as they would like, and they want to be involved in the lives of their children even at a distance.

For older adults who remain in the job market—or are displaced from a job and are seeking work—computer literacy is a necessity, not an option. Individuals who look for work, particularly those in clerical or administrative positions, must learn to use computers or be forced into unskilled and low-paying service jobs.

There are, of course, a large majority of older adults who are not early adopters of new technologies and have not learned how to use computers. But one can speculate that older adults will be willing to use them once their value has been demonstrated. The SeniorNet study (Adler, 1996) found that the use of high-tech products historically considered "cutting edge" was almost as high among these older Americans as among the general population. Among the respondents, 89 percent owned a microwave oven, 74 percent owned a VCR, and 62 percent subscribed to cable TV. The longer the product has been available, the more likely it is that older Americans will incorporate it into their lives.

Older Learners and Computer Technology

Educators of older adults have an interesting opportunity—and some challenges—as they meet the educational needs of older people who want to learn how to use computers. The opportunity is there to harness the technology and use it in new ways to design interactive instruction and further learning. But since the large majority of older adults are not yet computer literate, the immediate challenge is to provide learning experiences for computer novices.

The seemingly obvious way for older people to learn how to use a computer is to enroll in computer classes with people of all ages. But this is far from an ideal situation because most computer classes are designed for job-related training. Research in adult learning theory and practice indicates that reaction time slows as people age, and more time is needed to learn by rote and to process information. We also know that older adults learn well in a learning environment that allows for self-paced instruction; this principle is especially applicable for those who must learn to use unfamiliar high-tech equipment. There are also some attitudinal barriers that need to be overcome; many older adults are uneasy about trying their hand at a computer, and need an opportunity to build their confidence and self-esteem.

Barriers to Learning. We have come a long way since books like *Never Too Old to Learn* (Academy for Educational Development, 1974) were published. Our society, for the most part, has accepted the concept that older adults can and want to learn. Elderhostel and community-based adult learning programs are now a part of the American landscape. But many older people believe they are "too old" to learn the computer. This attitude stems, in many ways, from unfamiliarity with and anxiety about new technology. The fear of hitting the wrong key and then being unable to make corrections, or even breaking the computer, can be paralyzing for people of all ages, and particularly older adults. Embarrassment is another emotional barrier. Many older men, particularly those in management or the professions, relied on their female secretaries to type their correspondence; they never had experience with a keyboard and never felt it was appropriate to learn. Learning keyboarding as well as the technology from fast-paced instructors in a class full of young adults is a humbling and, for some, a threatening experience.

Remembering the operating instructions such as turning on the computer, using the mouse, naming and saving files, and printing documents can prove to be difficult for some older adults. Older people may experience some short-term memory loss and, coupled with computer anxiety, may have a difficult time remembering the seemingly illogical steps required to operate the computer.

It takes manual dexterity to click the mouse keys and maneuver the cursor on the screen; instructors report that while some older learners grasp the technology quickly, a significant number has some difficulty; arthritis and stiffness of joints play a part in this. Visual acuity declines with age, and eye strain that results in using the computer screen is not an uncommon problem. And many older adults experience physical discomfort from sitting at the computer for any long period of time.

The teaching methodology that works best for those older adults who are having difficulty grasping the technology is one that is nonthreatening and allows for some self-paced instruction. Rather than rushing through a standard curriculum, instructors must be prepared to have patience and to provide individual help. Computer lab time, with coaches present, permits the slower learners to have individual assistance and to use the equipment at their own pace. Peer instruction is recommended by some programs, but this is effective only if the peers understand how adults learn. In some cases, the peers might be engineers or "techies"; they may be excellent technicians, but simply unequipped to teach slower learners.

Once older learners master the basics, they become empowered. Instructors notice a renewed self-confidence and strong self-image. Perhaps they are exhilarated that they have accomplished a feat that they once considered the domain of the younger generation. They become a part of the "now" generation, and are not left behind their children, grandchildren, and younger friends and neighbors.

Model Educational Programs

Older adult education programming must appeal to the marketplace. Administrators offer courses and workshops to meet the demand. If the demand exists for particular subject areas, new classes are scheduled to fill the need. If few people participate, classes must be canceled.

Given the attention to computers in the press and in electronic media, it is not surprising that there is a strong demand for computer instruction for older adults. It is difficult to meet the demand because of the lack of availability of classrooms that have computer systems available; and students cannot learn how to use computers unless they have hands-on experience (one computer per student is necessary for optimal learning to take place). Some creative arrangements are being made with computer labs on campuses, private computer schools, and elementary and secondary schools so that older adults can learn in off-peak hours. But these programs reach only a small percentage of potential learners.

Educational programs to teach people who live in institutional settings such as continuing care retirement communities, assisted living facilities, and nursing homes to use computers—particularly to go online—have also been successfully initiated. Obtaining computer equipment is often the stumbling block for those in charge of programs and activities. And some professionals in these institutions do not have a vision of the positive effect that Internet access in particular might have on their residents.

One way to extend the reach so that broader numbers of older people can learn about computers is to offer demonstrations and lectures to provide an overview. This method, while no substitute for hands-on instruction, offers people a taste of the world of computer technology to see if they might like to pursue it further. It is also used as a marketing tool by the private sector to reach people who might be inspired to purchase computers at a later date.

For some older people, learning how to use a computer is not a discretionary activity. These are people who have been displaced from the job market and need to continue working in order to maintain their income. When people over age 55 seek work, they often find two hurdles to overcome: one is their age, and the other is their lack of computer technology skills. Programs have been developed specifically to train older people to use computers so they can get jobs.

Two programs are highlighted below: SeniorNet Learning Centers and Microsoft/American Association of Retired Persons (AARP) Community Technology Seminars. The SeniorNet Learning Centers offer computer instruction in 125 community-based settings. The Community Technology Seminars introduce older people to computing and to online services.

Two other programs deserving recognition are the Annenberg Pal Project (Wendt, Cody, Seymour, and Merrell, 1997), a two-year project based at the University of Southern California studying older adults and their use of the Internet in retirement and assisted living homes as well as in their own homes; and the Senior Community Service Employment Program, authorized by Title V of the Older Americans Act and funded by the Department of Labor, which provides computer training and job placement for low-income seniors in hundreds of sites around the country and is administered by national aging organizations such as AARP and the National Council of Senior Citizens.

SeniorNet. The earliest pioneer in computer instruction for older adults is SeniorNet, a national nonprofit organization based in San Francisco, and it continues to be a leader in teaching older people how to use computers and online services. Founded in 1987 as a research demonstration project by Dr. Mary Furlong, a professor of education at the University of San Francisco, SeniorNet now has twenty-two thousand members, has an online community on the World Wide Web, and sponsors 125 SeniorNet Learning Centers where older adults can learn how to use computers and computer technology.

The learning model that SeniorNet has developed and tested brings together elements of other successful peer-taught instructional programs for older adults. The SeniorNet model consists of these components: small classes, dedicated space with designated time set aside for computer lab work, computer coaches who tutor and work with students on a one-to-one basis, curriculum that is clearly written and permits self-pacing, eight-week classes, and use of peer instructors who are volunteers and who have completed a train-the-trainer program. Each learning center is run by an advisory board consisting of a volunteer coordinator and others who are in charge of various aspects of learning center administration, such as instruction, fund-raising, enrollment, and publicity.

The funding model for SeniorNet Learning Centers is unique as well. The learning centers are housed in community-based agencies such as senior centers, hospitals, community centers, and colleges. Paid staff from these sites serve as sponsors and are usually involved in the operations. The costs of establishing a learning center include start-up fees from the national office of SeniorNet for training, curriculum and technical assistance, and the acquisition of a minimum of ten computer systems. Companies such as IBM, which recognize the growing market of older computer users, have provided funds for establishing the learning centers and buying equipment for many of them. The IBM Learning Centers are generally located in places where a large number of IBM retirees reside. The retirees are then asked to serve as volunteer leaders and instructors. Other corporations, especially those involved in communication technology, have funded SeniorNet Learning Centers too.

The sites where SeniorNet Learning Centers are established reap many benefits in addition to meeting the needs of their constituency. Senior centers nationally are finding that their users are becoming older and more frail. A program like SeniorNet attracts the young-old and the more affluent, who may in turn volunteer and support other senior center programs. For hospitals, older computer learners represent a generally healthy clientele. By bringing them into the facility and exposing them to the hospital, it is anticipated that they may become supporters and potential users of the hospital's services. For all sites, the publicity generated by the learning center is very positive. The image of older people using what is often perceived as a young person's technology is attractive to journalists and the general public.

When a learning center is set up, demand exceeds supply. Because equipment is limited and classes are small, one article in a local newspaper can generate long waiting lists. Many senior centers and colleges understand the demand and, deciding not to affiliate with SeniorNet, have developed their own type of computer learning programs.

Initially, SeniorNet found that older adults came to the learning centers for a variety of reasons—a main reason was to learn word processing so they could write letters or memoirs. But as time has gone on, many new students sign up for courses because they want to find out about the Internet and how to use it.

Some older adults have come to the learning centers seeking help in learning job-related software for such occupations as accounting and medical office administration. A few of the learning centers have developed special programs to meet these needs. In the Norwalk, Connecticut, senior center, older adults who complete course work and become proficient at the computer can then sign up for job placement services.

Microsoft Community Technology Seminars. With the shortage of government and foundation funding, many nonprofit and academic institutions must be creative and seek partnerships in order to fund new programs and projects. Public-private partnerships seem logical for adult educators seeking to teach older people how to use computers since equipment is so expensive and becomes obsolete so quickly. Private hardware and software companies still think of younger markets when they think of computer instruction—perhaps because their employees tend to be under age 40—but they have as much to gain from an alliance as nonprofits do. Older adults have been identified as a new market by many computer companies—they are seen as potential buyers of hardware and software and users of Internet services.

Demonstrations and seminars to introduce older adults to the world of computing reach more people than classroom instruction and thus have a particular appeal. The expectation is that once people understand how a computer works and how easy it is to use, they will be more likely to purchase a computer system.

Microsoft and AARP have launched a joint venture, Community Technology Seminars, which are directed to AARP members to introduce them to computers and what they do. Five hundred seminars are taking place (between September 1997 and June 1998), each reaching a maximum of one hundred people. The purpose is "to help educate AARP members on the benefits of computer technology in their daily lives" (AARP, 1997). The seminar offers tips on buying a computer and using resources including the Internet; AARP's Webplace [http://www.aarp.org/index.html] is featured. Half of the seminars are geared to non-computer-users whereas the other half are geared to beginners interested in learning more. Microsoft is responsible for hiring and training seminar leaders, with consultation from AARP on how to teach older adults.

There is great interest in the seminars among AARP members. Both AARP and Microsoft have something to gain from their success; Microsoft can sell its software and AARP can provide education and promote the information and services on its web site.

Future Trends and Issues

Educators of adults have been involved for some time in experimenting with new technologies, telecommunications, and learning. But despite predictions that these technologies would change the face of learning, they have yet to make a great impact on how learning is delivered to older adults. Few older adults are significantly involved in distance learning.

We also need to analyze the relative failure of home study (print, audio, or video) and the older adult education market. Although many older people are self-directed learners who might relish the idea of taking courses on CD-ROM or online, learning in a classroom setting is a social as well as a growth experience for many older learners. One of the main reasons that older adults enroll in courses is to meet others who share their interests. Home study can be an isolating experience, except for the highly motivated.

There are some important differences between home study and computer-assisted instruction, however; one is the capacity for regular interaction in online curricula that is difficult if not impossible in traditional home study modes. The virtual classroom has great potential to attract older computer users and meet their needs both for growth and for socialization; this is particularly true for those people who are homebound due to physical disabilities, who are caring for others at home and find it difficult to attend classes, or who want to participate in night-time activities but do not drive at night. Garmer and Firestone (1996) found that "technology-based materials, which can be modularized and self-paced to respond to individual learning needs, offer unlimited opportunities for collaborative learning among groups and individuals working together to solve problems and reach common goals."

A major impediment to development of online and multimedia courses for older adults is their production cost. The development of computer-based instruction at the present time is market-driven; that is, the private sector will develop educational software and CD-ROMs if the market for them is apparent. The K–12 market is an example. Software for children has distribution channels through school systems and is also purchased by parents.

Inroads in computer-based instruction are also being made in corporate America. Training Divisions of the Fortune 500 companies are experimenting with new forms of learning such as interactive CD-ROM courses, Internet-based training on private areas, online collaborative learning, and other innovative uses of information technology. Many of the courses are designed for self-study, with the built-in incentive of job advancement or the earning of continuing professional education units to maintain certification with occupation groups. The private sector earmarks financial and human resources to develop, test, and evaluate new modes of instruction.

This is not the case in adult education. Costs to develop computer-based instruction are beyond the reach of adult education programs at the present time. The typical cost to produce an instructional CD-ROM is $100,000 for a two- to three-hour course. The adult education system, because it is so fragmented, would not be considered a viable market for private producers. Those educators and gerontologists who predict that lifelong learning is a growth industry as the baby boomers age need to show how computer technologies can be used before much investment will be made in older adult course development.

A recent research project finds a distinction between older people who use the Internet and the World Wide Web without using computers for other purposes and those who use computers for word processing, games, managing personal finances, and desktop publishing. "The internet and the world wide web have added a new dimension to the market for computers and created the market for newly developed internet appliances (i.e., WebTV). Rather than competing for the attention of the same people, these items appeal to different groups of people with identifiable characteristics" (Wendt, Cody, Seymour, Merrell, 1997). The majority of researchers have not made this distinction, painting a more holistic picture. The future will tell the story as marketers of WebTV promote Internet access independently from the sale of computer systems. At this writing, WebTV costs the consumer much less than a computer system. One can purchase WebTV for approximately $200 and then pay a monthly Internet access fee.

The principle of WebTV, which delivers the Internet through the TV screen, is similar to that of cable TV. Users receive a remote control device to access the Internet and a special keyboard to write e-mail messages. But other functions common to the computer such as word processing and record keeping are not available. If older people simply want to surf the net and write and receive e-mail and have no other uses for a computer, then WebTV is adequate for their needs. On the other hand, the more curious learner may find devices like WebTV too limiting. As the baby boomers age, the next cohorts will become more sophisticated technologically and will want computer systems not only for Internet access but also for broader purposes such as writing letters and tracking their finances, and they may prefer an office setting to a living room environment.

Educators of older adults do have some opportunities with WebTV that might not be possible with computers alone. For example, they might use it as an educational tool to connect groups of people, particularly those who are institutionalized, with the larger world outside. One might envision a class in a retirement community or nursing home (these facilities all have television sets) that teaches residents how to compose e-mail to their grandchildren and shows them attractive web sites that focus on areas of interest such as travel and health.

Adult educators have been concerned for some time about the people who will be left behind as information technology becomes more central to our lives—the disenfranchised, people with disabilities, and the many older adults who cannot afford to purchase computers. The relatively lower cost and ease of use of WebTV may address some of these concerns, enabling more people to access the Internet.

But WebTV is not a panacea. It does not meet the need, for example, of people with visual impairments who are denied access to some computer technology because of their disabilities. As personal computers become more important in the home and office, older people who are visually challenged need to have equal access. There have been some positive developments toward standardizing adaptive technology, primarily because of the mandates of the Americans with Disabilities Act (ADA) and because of the initiatives of leading personal computer software developers such as Microsoft. Adaptive computer software enables the magnification of printed text or the voice output of text. The Lighthouse National Center on Vision and Aging recommends that "libraries, senior centers, and community colleges—any institution offering computer or Internet classes to older adults—should be mindful of problems associated with age-related eye disorders. Adapting computer terminals and curriculum for this user population must be a fundamental consideration when planning educational training or programs" (Stuen, 1997). Recommendations for accommodating visually impaired older people include creating web sites that feature large type and color contrast, and offering text-only options or descriptions of graphics.

Knowledge of the computer and the Internet is an empowering experience for the older adults, for it keeps them connected to today's society and the future as well. Adult educators who expose those older adults who are isolated, poor, disabled, or less educated to computer technologies will help to enhance their lives.

The Internet has the amazing potential to provide information in an interesting way and to create a place where older adults from all over the country can form virtual "study circles" and self-help groups. Already, we see many examples. Organizations such as the Alzheimer's Association, AARP, and SeniorNet provide places online for older people who are caring for spouses and other family members. They receive educational information and learn from experts. Perhaps most important, they form self-help groups by using message boards to share their sorrows and joys, give caregiving tips, and offer words of encouragement to others who are in similar situations.

The Metropolitan Life Insurance Company, in combination with Senior-Net, has developed the MetLife Solutions Forum on SeniorNet where adults 55 and over come together to discuss issues of national concern and offer positive solutions. It was designed to give older people an opportunity to share their wisdom and experience and affect public policy. The solutions forum on the future of Medicare generated some cogent and creative suggestions. The participants had many ideas about ways to eliminate fraud, waste, and abuse and to change policies to care for those in need while keeping the Medicare system solvent for future generations (SeniorNet, 1997).

Third Age Media, a private, for-profit company with a web site [Thirdage.com] designed especially for people over age 50, presents useful information in a lively way and allows visitors to the site to meet each other, talk to experts online, and discuss almost any topic they choose. The company is financed by venture capital and corporate investment funds and expects to become profitable by attracting advertisers who wish to reach active and educated older computer users.

For the most part, the better-educated baby boomers are already knowledgeable about computers and the Internet. Computers are a part of their workplace and are integral to their children's education. As they reach age 55 and beyond, they will differ from earlier cohorts in that they will not need to learn the basics of computing or how to surf the Internet.

In addition, computers have become more user friendly, and this trend will certainly continue, enabling people to learn on their own. Already, most older people are self-taught on the computer; Adler, in a SeniorNet study, found that 39 percent taught themselves and 21 percent learned at work (1996). Help in installing and setting up the computer can be obtained not through an educational institution but by contacting computer stores or computer consultants.

What, then, is the older adult educator's future role in computer technology? The focus will not be on teaching people computer basics. The challenge will be a bigger one—to integrate older learners, especially older women who have traditionally not been computer users and others who do not have access, into the world of computer technology so they can be full participants with the rest of society in the information age. Negroponte speculates that "some people worry about the social divide between the information-rich and the information-poor, the haves and the have-nots, the First and the Third Worlds. But the real cultural divide is going to be generational" (1996). Will older people lose their place in society and will their quality of life decrease because of their exclusion from the digital age?

Another challenge will be to experiment with new modes of instruction, taking advantage of a medium that seems to promote self-directed learning and that also allows older people to come together in virtual communities to access information and to learn from each other. Some of Candy's (1991) recommendations to evaluate and then assist adults to become self-directed learners can easily be applied in the information age. Older adult educators may find that their role is one of advocate and facilitator as older adults cautiously approach the information superhighway. And they may make their greatest contribution by recruiting older adults as "cyberdocents" who are technologically savvy and skilled at the computer to teach and coach their peers, to manage message boards and web sites, and to develop new ways to use the technology for older adult learning.

References

Academy for Educational Development. *Never Too Old to Learn.* A report submitted to the Edna McConnell Clark Foundation. New York: Academy for Educational Development, 1974.

Adler, R. P. *Older Adults and Computers: Report of a National Survey.* Report. San Francisco: SeniorNet [http:///www.seniornet.org./intute/survey1.html], 1996.

American Association of Retired Persons (AARP). "Microsoft Community Technology Seminars." Internal memo, June 30, 1997.

Candy, P. C. *Self-Direction for Lifelong Learning: A Comprehensive Guide to Theory and Practice.* San Francisco: Jossey-Bass, 1991.

Garmer, A. K., and Firestone, C. M. *Creating a Learning Society: Initiatives for Education and Technology.* A Report of the Aspen Institute Forum on Communications and Society. Washington, D.C.: The Aspen Institute, 1996.

Katz, K. "The Third Age Online: A Quantitative Analysis." Paper presented at Business Forum on Aging of the American Society on Aging/Third Age Media Conference, New York, Sep. 25, 1997.

Negroponte, N. *Being Digital.* New York: Alfred A. Knopf, 1996.

SeniorNet. *MetLife Solutions Forum on SeniorNet. In Their Own Words: Seniors Discuss the Future of Medicare.* Report on Forum 1. San Francisco: SeniorNet, 1997.

Stuen, C. "Older Adults and the Information Age." *Aging & Vision News,* Spring 1997, 8.

Third Age Media and the Excite Network. "Excite and Thirdage.com Host Pioneering Psychographic Study of Web Users." Redwood City, Calif., Excite, Inc. [http://corp.excite.com/press/092597/thirdage.html], 1997.

Wendt, P. F., Cody, M. J., Seymour, R., and Merrell, T. "Annenberg Pal Project: Older Adults on the Internet." University of Southern California, Ethel Percy Andrus Gerontology Center Web Site [http://www.usc.edu/dept/gero/research/annenberg.shtml], 1997.

SANDRA TIMMERMANN, ED.D., is director of the Mature Market Institute at Metropolitan Life Insurance Company.

Although individuals age differently, they also share a group identity as part of a cohort-group with a common social history. The schemata used in this chapter reflects the influence of such common histories on learning needs, interests, and styles in older adulthood.

Cohorts of the Future

C. Joanne Grabinski

"Silents Journey into Landscape of Old Age." "Boomers Grow Old." "13ers Age." "Millenials Come of Old Age." So headlines read as these generations arrive at older adulthood. Although each member of a generation has an individual life trajectory, members of each cohort-group also have a common history because they live through similar societal events at similar ages. This common socialization results in a generational "peer personality" (Strauss and Howe, 1991).

Demographers describe cohorts as individuals born the same year or within the same five-to-ten-year period. Family social scientists and genealogists use the concept of generations to describe layers of a family tree. Strauss and Howe (1991), through their synonymous use of the terms "cohort-groups," "generations," and "cohort generations," blend the concepts of generation and age cohort in formulating a Theory of Generations across historical time (1589–2069) in America. *Generation* refers to a cohort-group whose age boundaries are set by its peer personality rather than by strict chronological birth years (p. 60). Four of their eighteen generations—"Silents," "Boomers," "13ers," and "Millenials"—are the older Americans with and for whom we will develop educational experiences. Useful insights into learning needs, interests, and styles of these generations are gained through the Theory of Generations conceptual framework.

Life Phases and Central Social Roles

Strauss and Howe describe four "life phases," twenty-two years per phase (see Table 7.1), and suggest a "central social role" for each phase:

Table 7.1. Cohort-Groups

	Birth	Elderhood	Late elderhood
Silents	1925–1942	1991–2008	2017–2030
Boomers	1943–1960	2009–2026	2031–2048
13ers (thirteeners)	1961–1981	2027–2047	2049–2069
Millenials	1982–2005	2048–2071	2070–2093

Source: Adapted from Strauss and Howe, 1991.

Elderhood (age 66 to 87). Central role: stewardship (supervising, mentoring, channeling endowments, passing on values).

Midlife (age 44 to 65). Central role: leadership (parenting, teaching, directing institutions, using values).

Rising adulthood (age 22 to 43). Central role: activity (working, starting families and livelihoods, serving institutions, testing values).

Youth (age 0 to 21). Central role: dependence (growing, learning, accepting protection and nurture, avoiding harm, acquiring values). (1991, pp. 60–61)

Of primary concern herein is elderhood. With an increasing number of Americans living into their 90s and 100s, however, a fifth life phase, late elderhood (age 88 to 109), should be added. The challenge, then, is to identify a central social role for late elderhood; three excellent candidates are "life review" (Butler, 1996), "preservation of self" (Tobin, 1991), and "vital involvement" (Erikson, Erikson, and Kivnick, 1986).

Peer Personality

Strauss and Howe (1991) posit that each generation develops a *peer personality:* "a generational persona recognized and determined by (1) common age location; (2) common beliefs and behavior; and (3) perceived membership in a common generation" (p. 64). Peer personality "distinguishes a generation as a cohesive cohort-group with its own unique biography" and portrays "collective attitudes a generation has about family life, sex roles, institutions, politics, religion, lifestyle, and the future" (p. 63).

Social Moment

A generation's peer personality is shaped by the "social moment(s)" in which generation members are socialized (during youth and, perhaps, rising adulthood) and begin to recognize the impact of historic events on their social environment (Strauss and Howe, 1991, p. 71). Two social moment eras occur: "*secular crises,* when society focuses on reordering the outer world of institutions and public behavior; and *spiritual awakenings,* when society focuses on changing the inner world of values and private behavior" (p. 71). These moments alternate regularly; each lasts two life phases (forty to forty-five years).

Generational Types

Strauss and Howe (1991) describe a fixed-order, recurring cycle of four generational types, alternately labeled as dominant or recessive, that further clarifies peer personality:

Idealist: dominant, inner-fixated; spiritual awakening in youth and rising adulthood, secular crisis in rising adulthood and elderhood; "prophetic life cycle of vision and values" (pp. 74–75).

Reactive: recessive; spiritual awakening in youth, secular crisis in rising adulthood and midlife, spiritual awakening in elderhood; "picaresque lifestyle of survival and adventure" (pp. 74–75).

Civic: dominant, outer-fixated; secular crisis in youth and rising adulthood; spiritual awakening in midlife and elderhood; "heroic life cycle of secular achievement and reward" (pp. 74–75).

Adaptive: recessive; secular crisis in youth, spiritual awakening in rising adulthood and midlife, secular crisis in elderhood; "genteel life cycle of expertise and amelioration" (pp. 74–75).

So, what does all this mean for Silents, Boomers, 13ers, and Millenials? The following discussion focuses on sociohistorical factors that shape each generation's peer personality and draws implications from them for professional practice in older adult education.

Silents

Born 1925–1942; 56 to 73 years old in 1998; will enter elderhood in 1991–2008, and late elderhood in 2017–2030. Generational type: recessive adaptive (Strauss and Howe, 1991). Archetype: Artist, characterized as overprotected children, sensitive young adults, indecisive midlife leaders, empathic elders (Strauss and Howe, 1997, p. 84).

Peer Personality. Silents are children of the Great Depression and World War II, a small generation wedged between "doer" G.I.s and "love child" Boomers. As young adults, they attended college, entered the Peace Corps, and became activists and leaders in the Civil Rights Movement, producing "virtually every major figure in the modern civil rights movement" (Strauss and Howe, 1991, p. 284). They created the surge of growth in the helping professions (teaching, medicine, ministry, and government) and in public-interest advocacy groups. In politics and business, Silents are "bureaucratizers." They have produced first ladies, but, to their dismay, not presidents (p. 285).

Silents are the "earliest-marrying and earliest-babying" (Strauss and Howe, 1991, p. 284) of any American generation. "Cashless" as children, they have moved quickly and smoothly to "the cusp of affluent elderhood" (p. 284). College-graduate males became the "gray-flannel executives." Silent females often entered male-only fields in college, then opted for marriage and children over careers. Twenty years later, however, most of the nation's prominent feminists were Silent females. Silents also caught the brunt of the "sexual revolution" and "divorce epidemic" (p. 284).

Although their resumes support the notion that Silents are the establishment, they have a tremendous sense of "power inadequacy" (Strauss and Howe, 1991, p. 291). Their leadership seems focused more on "deferring or learning to live with problems than [on] taking aggressive steps to solve them" (p. 291). Their decisions and contributions frequently are described as "perfect but wrong"; such judgment fosters "a wounded collective ego" (p. 292).

Confused about their purpose and feeling vaguely dissatisfied with jobs, families, and self, they are snapping up early retirement incentives—often without a clue about what comes next (p. 292).

To their credit, Silents' legacy includes their strength in using personal communication to get others to solve conflicts; their willingness to give to others (from familial obligations to other people's charities); their focus on process rather than end product or outcome; and their leadership in the transition from nuclear age to information age (Strauss and Howe, 1991).

Practice Implications. Silents are an educated generation—most completed high school; many earned college degrees. They actively pursue further professional and advanced academic opportunities. Silents are leaders in the development of professional standards, certification, licensure, and accreditation. They seem to prefer formal educational opportunities planned by others over self-guided or informal learning. They like to discuss, so discussion-based programming such as Great Decisions, Town Halls, and book clubs should continue to flourish. As the G.I.s before them currently show considerable interest in "reminiscence-style" educational opportunities about the Great Depression and World War II, Silents should enjoy similar educational programs about the Civil Rights Movement.

As activists, they will seek educational programming to support their volunteerism and post-retirement employment. Having jumped on the early-retirement bandwagon, many Silents will have trouble adjusting to a nonworking status and may not be completely satisfied with volunteering. This suggests the need for career counseling, job retraining, and recruitment to degree and vocational programs to prepare them for new jobs.

Silents like to travel, so programs such as Elderhostel should continue, although there is a need to develop Elderhostel-like programming for low-income elders and those who are homebound or confined to long-term care settings. Silents enjoy interactive television programming, Internet courses, and other distance-learning options if they are truly interpersonal and interactive.

As caregivers for aging parents, siblings, and spouses, as well as for children and grandchildren, Silents need education about caregiving, parenting grandchildren, disease processes, accessing medical care systems, and health consumerism. As outer-driven individuals, Silents are more likely to participate in such programs if they are other-focused (not self-focused) and also have a support group component.

Since rote learning was the primary mode of learning in childhood, Silents may prefer educational experiences that use rote strategies. This also helps to overcome stereotypes about memory loss in old age; they can "use it" instead of "lose it." Many went through elementary school in multigrade classrooms, so Silents are good candidates for age-integrated learning environments. Among the first to experience college-prep formats in high school, they will appreciate preparatory orientation, learning, and guidance sessions prior to entering intensive or long-term learning programs.

Boomers

Born 1943–1960; 38 to 55 years old in 1998; will enter elderhood in 2009–2026 and late elderhood in 2031–2048. Generational type: dominant idealist (Strauss and Howe, 1991). Archetype: Prophet, characterized as indulged youth, narcissistic young adult crusaders, moralistic midlifers, wise elders (Strauss and Howe, 1997, p. 84).

Peer Personality. The boom generation seems a perfect match for its idealist generational type. At each life phase thus far, they have been the most watched generation ever—the "cultural and spiritual focal point for American society" (Strauss and Howe, 1991, p. 301). This is a large, well-recognized and influential cohort-group that even had its own generational pediatrician—Dr. Spock! Boomers have grown up not just with TV, but on TV. Across their lifespan, "they have metamorphosed from Beaver Cleaver to hippie to braneater to yuppie to . . . 'Neo-Puritan'" (p. 299). Seemingly chameleon, they have had more temporary labels than any other generation—just add the word "generation" to "Pepsi," "rock," "Woodstock," "sixties," "Vietnam," "me," "love," "yuppie," and many other terms (p. 299).

Indulged by parents and communities with great expectations for them, Boomers turned to self-absorption. First-wave Boomers ("Victory babies") are the most self-absorbed, while last-wavers "show Boomish streaks of intellectual arrogance and social immaturity" (Strauss and Howe, 1991, p. 301). Coined during the Vietnam War, the term "post-adolescence" captured society's image of Boomers as adolescents "stuck in the sixties" (p. 301). Within families, Boomers were closely attached to mothers, but they revolted against G.I. fathers during the generation gap of the "consciousness revolution." Their actions, symbols, and ethos during and after the generation gap "remained a deliberate antithesis to everything G.I.: spiritualism over science, gratification over patience, negativism over positivism, fractiousness over conformity, rage over friendliness, *self over community*" (p. 302).

During rising adulthood, the central theme of Boomers was "quest for self" (Strauss and Howe, 1991, p. 302), outwardly manifested by "a sense of suspended animation, . . . resistance to permanent linkages (mates, children, corporations, professions)," social grazing, a "pick-and-choose idealism, . . . an apparent lack of interest in building community life," and development of "a unique brand of perfectionism in consumption" (p. 302). They were into "zen luxuriousness." Observers saw a mix of high self-esteem and selective self-indulgence dressed in counterculture clothing and ideals (p. 303).

Their self-fixation led Boomers to use internal standards and an unwavering sense of right and wrong to shape their plans, decisions, and judgments. Their preference for deductive logic "has made Boomers better philosophers than scientists, better preachers than builders" (Strauss and Howe, 1991, p. 303). Their career preferences are meaningful, creative, and independent (p. 302); for example, they have chosen careers in the media and small, home-based businesses (p. 311).

Seeing themselves as "the embodiment of moral wisdom," midlife Boomers appear to be "growing up to a new sense of responsibility and self-denial" and a "new seriousness" (Strauss and Howe, p. 312). They continue, however, to operate more on individual, parallel pathways than from a collective stance. With an increasing tendency toward severity, they prefer destruction over mere defeat of enemies (p. 314). More interested in fostering crisis than solving it and fascinated with "apocalyptic solutions," Boomers push for "more explicit exercise of public authority" (more taxes, zoning, schools, prisons, and capital punishment) and defend conservative values (monogamy, thrift, abstention from drugs) (p. 315).

Practice Implications. With Boomers still in midlife (eleven years away from elderhood) and their drastic turn from hippie to yuppie, it is difficult to speculate about the nature of educational opportunities older adult Boomers will seek. In childhood and adolescence, school curricula valued skills over subject matter; social relevance took priority over timeless facts. This suggests an interest in how-to learning focused on ideas and ideals rather than products. As idealists with a prognosis to emerge as visionary guides for the next secular crisis, Boomers may prefer to be teachers rather than students. Their strong interest in values, morals, spirituality, and psychic phenomena suggests course content related to rules, regulations, and laws. It is a foregone conclusion they will not like activities that end with just one correct answer! If a learning group involves both first-and late-wave Boomers, debate will occur; program designers and instructors should use such debate as a learning strategy. With their insistence on meaningful experience, programs and courses must have well-defined goals, objectives, and outcomes relevant for each individual student.

Much has been written about problems Boomers will face because of their apparent inability to plan and save for retirement. Also, they may not have pension funds, Social Security, and Medicare as we know them today. If so, educational programs about establishing or maintaining financial security, inexpensive healthcare options, and vocational retraining programs are necessary. Because of their focus on self, however, Boomers probably will prefer individualized learning packets and self-study experiences over classroom-based courses developed for groups.

Their poor track record with interpersonal and marital relationships might lead elderly Boomers to seek combined education-counseling programs to help them in developing new, more meaningful relationships. Certainly, education about how to live with long-term consequences of the "free love" and "drug" culture will be appropriate.

Boomer SAT scores declined drastically and dropping out of school and society was frequent. Boomer dropouts might be ready to play catch-up; if so, high school completion and college degree programs designed specifically for their interests are needed. Traditional learning institutions and programs, however, may not be their schools of choice. In this light, note that teachers and administrators for the alternative high school and charter school movements are Boomers, and laws to create such alternatives are being forged by Boomer governors and legislators. This provides clues about the type of learning environments they might prefer.

13ers (Thirteeners)

Born 1961–1981; 17 to 37 years old in 1998; will enter elderhood in 2027–2047 and late elderhood in 2049–2069. Generational type: recessive reactive (Strauss and Howe, 1991). Archetype: Nomad, characterized as under-protected children, alienated young adults, pragmatic midlife leaders, tough elders (Strauss and Howe, 1997, p. 84).

Peer Personality. As the "true children of the 1960s" (Strauss and Howe, 1991, p. 321), 13ers, especially first-wavers, have had to live with and survive whatever Boomers left behind. Those "leftovers" include low test scores, high crime rates, increasing suicide rates, and substance abuse. Their social moment events include the chaos of Vietnam, Three-Mile Island, and Christmas without lights (p. 317).

Thirteeners are the "most-aborted generation in American history" (Strauss and Howe, 1991, p. 324) and have been stung the worst by parental (and grandparental) divorce rates. They despair over lack of parental authority that they blame on family instability. Their complex family lives mean they might have lived with a single parent, shuttled back and forth between parental and step-parental homes, and tried to figure out how to relate with their parents' current and past spouses, significant others, lovers, and strangers at the breakfast table (pp. 325, 329).

During their K–12 education, 13ers experienced two major catch-22 situations. First, as they entered school, "educational experts and gurus" pronounced there was *not* an "indispensable body of knowledge that every child should know" (Strauss and Howe, 1991, p. 321). As 13ers graduated from high school, a new set of gurus announced there *was* such a body of knowledge, and 13ers had not learned it! Second, 13ers experienced the heyday of open classrooms and liked the freedom they provided. When evaluations showed open classrooms were the site of bad education, 13ers became skeptical about situations in which barriers are removed (p. 333).

As they reached high school, grade inflation was ending, taxpayers were revolting against school taxes, and school districts were hit with a budget crunch. Teachers in a 1980 study rated 13ers lower than Boomers on most measures of aptitude and achievement. Unless something changes, 13ers will be the first generation in a long time to be less college-educated than the generation before them (Strauss and Howe, 1991, p. 325). Male 13ers' preference for military service has provided the armed forces with the "best-educated generation of soldiers in American history" (p. 326).

Thirteeners have committed teen suicide more frequently than any previous generation and are the "most heavily incarcerated generation in American history" (Strauss and Howe, 1991, p. 326). Economically, they are the poorest among the four generations considered here. As a result, many 13ers still live in parental homes; most may never own a home (p. 327).

Thirteeners were told to "grow up fast" and to be "self-reliant, independent, self-actualizing individuals" (Strauss and Howe, 1991, p. 321). To do so, they carefully observed and emulated adult behavior, then became "the kind of kids adults have a hard time finding adorable" (p. 321). Compared to Boomer "post-adolescents" in rising adulthood, 13ers are "proto-adults" in adolescence (p. 321). Societally, they are branded as the alienated generation X and blamed for creating their own negative images as a "lost," "ruined," and "wasted" generation (Strauss and Howe, 1991, p. 317).

Thirteeners do not agree with these images. Instead, 13ers see themselves as "pragmatic, quick, sharp-eyed, able to step outside themselves to understand the game of life as it really gets played. And, whatever they are, 13ers insist, they *have* to be" (Strauss and Howe, 1991, p. 320).

Thirteeners fit well their reactive generational type. Underprotected and criticized as youth, they became alienated, but risk-taking, rising adults. They are forecast to be pragmatic midlife leaders; the pragmatism is already in place, but we are just beginning to catch a glimpse of their leadership. It may be this leadership, however, that finally allows them to set aside the "lost," "ruined," and "wasted" labels. They are survivors; it is this ability to cope and survive that will gain them, perhaps grudgingly, the respect Strauss and Howe foresee for them in elderhood.

Practice Implications. At 17 to 37 years of age, 13ers are still in their youth and rising adulthood life phases. It is difficult to look thirty to fifty years into the future to see what they will be like or what type of educational opportunities they will want as older adults. Instead, perhaps adult education professionals should consider what educational programming is needed to help 13ers survive through elderhood. True to their theme of pragmatism, 13ers will be most interested in education that maintains and enhances their coping and survival skills. Having lived in the shadow of Boomers and having been denigrated by them, 13ers may reject authority figures who are Boomers. This suggests the need for instructor and administrator training programs that address generational profiles and issues.

Thirteeners successful in traditional educational systems will continue to pursue formal education opportunities, including graduate school. Those not as successful, however, are likely to avoid traditional school programs and settings. Community colleges and vocational schools may be more comfortable learning environments than colleges and universities. Educators also should think creatively about delivering alternative programs in other settings—what about movie theaters, coffee shops,and bookstores? Strauss and Howe (1991) report 13ers are showing the first signs of generational peer bonding through "a common alienation visible in 13er art and music, and in their growing awareness of their own economic vulnerability" (p. 330). They also have published several generation X anthologies (essays, short stories, and poems). If this is where 13ers live, this is where we will educate!

Educational programming related to 13ers' vulnerabilities and problems is needed. For example, their poor economic status, "McJob" occupations rather than careers, and unstable housing situations suggest learning experiences about creative financing, tenants' rights, job retention, skill training, and income enhancement. Strauss and Howe (1991) suggest 13ers' "best chance of success comes from striking out on their own, finding a market niche, and filling it more cheaply and sensibly than older-run businesses" (p. 331). In this case, education about small business development, ownership, and growth would be appropriate. Health and fitness programs are needed, although 13ers might resist—especially if these are provided by Boomers. Not to be forgotten is their higher incidence of incarceration, which suggests that educational programs for 13ers "aging in place" will be a necessity.

Millenials

Born 1982–approximately 2005; not yet born to 16 years old in 1998; will enter elderhood in 2048–approximately 2071 and late elderhood in 2070–approximately 2093. Generational type: probably dominant, outer-fixated Civics (Strauss and Howe, 1991). Archetype: probably hero, characterized as protected children, heroic young adult team workers, energetic midlifers, powerful elders (Strauss and Howe, 1997, p. 84).

Peer Personality. Millenials are children their parents wanted to have! Abortion, voluntary sterilization, and divorce rates are down. Planned-for babies are celebrated at conception and birth. Family time at home is gaining renewed popularity (Strauss and Howe, 1991, p. 337). Fathers are demanding "daddytracks" at work to provide more time for involvement in child nurture (p. 338).

Disappointed at how 13ers turned out and with grave doubts about how 13ers were raised, older generations are moving quickly "to assert greater adult dominion over the world of childhood—and to implant civic virtue in a new crop of youngsters" (Strauss and Howe, 1991, p. 335). This is evident in ambitious educational goals for the year 2000 and the class of 2000, including the 90 percent graduation rate set by governors in 1990. The goal for American children to be number one in the world in science and math achievement is widely touted. Another goal is for a "smoke-free high school class of 2000" (p. 335). There is growing criticism of anti-child policies such as "unchecked growth in federal borrowing" and "dwindling health benefits for impoverished mothers" (pp. 337–338). The KIDS-PAC lobby has been formed.

Stronger, less ambivalent moral messages are being sent through "anti-campaigns" (against drugs, alcohol, AIDS, early sex, teen pregnancy, profanity, lurid music lyrics, TV ads, sex and violence on TV) to protect children and prevent the "sins" of the 13ers and Boomers (Strauss and Howe, 1991, p. 338). Instead of R-rated movies about kids, G-rated movies stressing "civic virtues (equality, optimism, cooperation, community)" (p. 338) are being made for kids. There is a serious effort to remove children from dangerous environments and to remove danger from the environments in which children live, study, and play. New child-safety products are flooding the market. State laws mandate and enforce use of child restraints in cars and airplanes; bicycle helmet laws have been enacted in many states (p. 339). Legislation is being enacted to remove children from jobs that endanger or exploit them.

"Ever so gradually, adults of all ages are rediscovering an affection and sense of public responsibility for other people's children" (Strauss and Howe, 1991, p. 339). Children are seen as precious, sometimes more so than their parents. Substance-abusing mothers are jailed for endangering their unborn children. New parental liability (civil and criminal) laws now hold parents responsible for their children's misdeeds (p. 339).

Schools are moving toward a "new traditionalism" that includes values, greater adult assertiveness, academic kindergartens, more homework, longer school days, tougher graduation requirements, and greater parental involvement in classrooms. There are calls for stronger national- and state-mandated standardized curricula and stricter testing of students and teachers. Courts are reversing student rights and strengthening school disciplinarians' roles. Down with "parents as pals" and parental permissiveness; up with firm rules enforced by adult supervision and appropriate punishment when transgressions occur (Strauss and Howe, 1991, pp. 340–341). PTAs are flourishing. Some are attempting to slow down the childhood developmental clock through testing for kindergarten readiness and holding children back when they have not met objective measures of achievement in academic and social skills (p. 340).

"The Millenials show every sign of being a generation of trends—toward improved education and health care, strengthening families, more adult affection and protection, and a rising sense that youths need a national mission" (Strauss and Howe, 1991, p. 341). If so, Millenials will increasingly resemble their G.I. generation great-grandparents. They will be the working-together scouts, warriors, and heroes in rising adulthood who, as powerful civic leaders in their midlife and later years, will build and restructure societal institutions.

Practice Implications. Although the oldest Millenials are just 16 years old in 1998 and not all Millenials have been born yet, it is possible to project their learning needs and interests when they enter elderhood and later elderhood. If they follow the Theory of Generations schemata, Millenials will be much like their G.I. generation great-grandparents. GIs currently are the backbone of Elderhostel and Institute for Learning in Retirement educational programs; Millenials should enjoy such programs if they are updated for relevancy in 2048 and beyond. As elders, Millenials will be interested in learning for the sake of learning. They will be prepared to study and will come to class prepared. If, as projected, they are healthier older adults, we should anticipate their interest in degree-granting programs for both professional and personal purposes.

Millenials' computer-proficiency began in pre-school days, and interactive television is a common classroom experience. They will expect access to educational opportunities that take full advantage of these and newer technological tools.

Millenials are children of the charter school movement, many of which have adopted an "integrated content" model of learning. This suggests Millenials will prefer multi- and interdisciplinary learning experiences. Internet and related technologies have provided them a global education; Millenials will want to continue educational travel (in person or via technology) into their later years.

Conclusion

Every cohort group or generation has its own unique niche in sociohistorical time. The strength of Strauss and Howe's (1991) theory of generations framework is that it allows us to take into account the life history and generational peer personality of each learner in any given educational experience. Also, we can gain useful clues about older adult learners through an understanding of the recurring cycle of generational types and alternating social moments.

In this chapter, only a taste of the framework and its use as an educational planning tool could be provided. A rewarding professional development experience would be a discussion group for teacher and administrator participants who study this framework and then use and evaluate it as a tool in their work with older adult learners. To take full advantage of the framework, however, teachers and administrators should identify which generation they belong to and consider how that influences their teaching or administrative styles.

References

Butler, R. N. "Life Review." In J. E. Birren (ed.), *Encyclopedia of Gerontology: Age, Aging, and the Aged (Vol. 2)*. San Diego: Academic Press, 1996.

Erikson, E. H., Erikson, J. M., and Kivnick, H. Q. *Vital Involvement in Old Age*. New York: Norton, 1986.

Strauss, W., and Howe, N. *Generations: The History of America's Future, 1584–2069*. New York: William Morrow, Inc., 1991.

Strauss, W., and Howe, N. *The Fourth Turning: An American Prophecy*. New York: Broadway Books, 1997.

Tobin, S. S. *Personhood in Advanced Old Age: Implications for Practice*. New York: Springer, 1991.

C. JOANNE GRABINSKI is president of AgeEd, a consulting firm specializing in education, training, and research on family and educational gerontology, and lecturer for the Gerontology Program at Eastern Michigan University.

McClusky's assessment of the role of education in the lives of older adults as "essentially an affirmative enterprise" is a theme that reappears throughout the chapters of this volume and promises to be more completely realized in the future study and practice of educational gerontology.

Epilogue

James C. Fisher, Mary Alice Wolf

A quarter century ago, Howard McClusky wrote about the role of education in the lives of older adults, describing it as "essentially an affirmative enterprise" likely to "lead to something better in the lives of those participating" (McClusky, 1973, p. 2). His optimism is echoed in the title of this book, *Using Learning to Meet the Challenges of Older Adulthood,* and is a persistent theme in its discussion on theoretical and research underpinnings on older adult learning and of the current programmatic manifestations and implications for future program and policy development. At many points, the literature on research and theory echoes the McClusky theme. A positive view of older adult learning is found in Mary Alice Wolf's presentation of the developmental potential of elders and in James C. Fisher's discussion of research findings that suggest an important role for adult educators in maintaining old abilities and in developing new ones.

McClusky's theme is also played out in the range of programs described in Chapter Four. Learning activities for this population are founded on a broader conceptual base than that provided by adult education alone, and the program activities are sponsored by a wide range of educational and social service institutions. The promise of programs currently available for older persons calls to mind the ubiquity of Elderhostel, Learning-in-Retirement, and Senior Center programs. One is challenged to identify an institution of higher education, an adult education facility, or a community recreation program that does not sponsor at least one such program especially for older adults. In fact, at least one community college boasts of serving more students in its Elderhostel programs than through its regular curriculum.

Yet one must also observe that despite the promise inherent in older adult learning, participation has increased only to 17 percent for those age 60 to 64 and to 10 percent for those 65 and over (Kopka and Peng, 1993). Although these represent increases of significant proportion over data reported in the 1970s and 1980s, the promise of a better life inherent in education for older adults is clearly not being materialized in over three-quarters of the population. With all of the conceptual support and evidence of available learning opportunities, David A. Peterson and Hiromi Masunaga assert that "few real innovations" in older adult education have occurred since the 1950s and that, citing Moody, "[t]he most important observation about education for older adults in America is that the enterprise is not serious" (see Peterson and Masunaga, Chapter Five). Peterson and Masunaga base these assertions in part on the dearth of any broad policies that directly support older adult learning enterprises.

Apart from those employed persons taking at least one employment-related course during the previous year, most courses were for personal/family/social reasons. Fewer than 1 percent of older persons cited training for a new job, improving basic skills, or obtaining a diploma or degree as reasons for participation (Kopka and Peng, 1993). The main focus of older adult learning activities on personal enrichment and socialization suggests that within the broad spectrum of educational opportunities, only a narrow band of learning needs are being addressed. Furthermore, an examination of the providers suggests that those most rapidly growing programs, Elderhostel and Learning-in-Retirement for example, cater to the preferences of older adults of above-average educational and socioeconomic status, indicating that from a program perspective, the "generation of persons in the later years who are models of lifelong fulfillment" anticipated by McClusky (1976, p. 11) is yet to be achieved in the fullest sense. Unfortunately, at present, the model learner anticipated by McClusky is comprised of a small part of the older adult population. One can only hope that the future cohorts described by C. Joanne Grabinski in Chapter Seven will reverse this trend.

Not surprising to adult educators, those who have traditionally succeeded in and benefitted from education as adults continue to do so in their later years. The potential for computer-based learning is acknowledged by Sandra Timmermann in Chapter Six; yet we do not know enough about this burgeoning world of cybertechnology to fully appreciate the role that it will play for older adults. In self-directed learning, social chat rooms, employment, and medical support, computers currently serve many older adults seeking information. How older-adult learning needs will influence into this paradigm and be influenced by it, we can only speculate.

One must conclude that a majority of the broader population fails to rely on conventional educational programs as important assists in meeting the challenges of older adulthood. Educational programs that produce skills in self-maintenance, in literacy, and in coping, receive less emphasis and less participation than those activities that focus on leisure. Certainly alternative program designs and varieties of self-directed learning strategies bear closer scrutiny as learning tools that older adults use to meet the challenges they face. Among the broad inventories of services necessary to address the needs of older persons, educational services usually rank far below social services. An important task is that of conveying the conviction that educational services support more than just leisure and enjoyment activities and contribute substantially to the psychological, sociological, economic, and physical well-being of older adults.

With program breadth, technological innovations, and broad conceptual and research support, the promise inherent in older adult learning has been realized in part. The task of building support to address the learning needs of an increasingly diverse older adult student population is before us. It has been the purpose of this volume to lay a groundwork for that effort and to provide a justification for the continuing work of research, theorybuilding, policy-making, technology use, and program development, with a view to engaging the older adult population in its broadest dimensions as learners.

References

Kopka, T.L.C., and Peng, S. S. "Adult Education: Main Reasons for Participating. Statistics in Brief." Washington, D.C.: U.S. Department Of Education, Office of Educational Research and Improvement, National Center for Education Statistics, 1993.

McClusky, H. Y. "Co-Chairman's Statement (Section on Education)." *Toward a National Policy on Aging.* Final report, Vol. II, White House Conference on Aging. Washington, D.C.: U.S. Government Printing Office, 1973.

McClusky, H. Y. "What Research Says About Adult Learning Potential and Teaching Older Adults." In R. M. Smith (ed.), *Adult Learning: Issues and Innovations.* DeKalb, Ill.: ERIC Clearinghouse in Career Education, Department of Secondary and Adult Education, Northern Illinois University, 1976. (ED 131 197)

JAMES C. FISHER *is associate professor of adult and continuing education at the University of Wisconsin–Milwaukee.*

MARY ALICE WOLF *is professor of human development and gerontology and director of the Institute on Gerontology at Saint Joseph College, West Hartford, Connecticut.*

INDEX

Academy for Educational Development, 63

Adair, S. R., 6, 34

Adler, R. P., 61, 70

Administration on Aging, 1, 50

Adult Education Association of the United States of America, 8

Alzheimer's Association, 70

American Association of Retired Persons (AARP), 1, 18, 47, 57, 65, 67, 70

Americans with Disabilities Act (ADA), 69

Annenberg Pal Project, 65

Apprentice programs, 45

Association for Gerontology and Higher Education (AGHE) Standards and Guidelines, 59

Baby boomers, 7, 70, 73, 77–79

Baker, A. J., 1

Baltes, P. B., 19

Bankhead, D. R., 33

Baron, A., 29

Bashore, T. R., 29

Bass, S. A., 20, 27

Beatty, P. T., 18, 19, 20, 41

Berg, C. A., 19

Besdine, R., 16, 19

Birren, J. E., 18, 19

Blazey, M. L., 27

Boggs, D. L., 18, 20

Bornat, J., 18

Bramwell, R. D., 11

Brockett, R. G., 6, 18, 20

Brown, H., 35

Brown, J. M., 36

Burnside, I., 18

Butler, D. Q., 33

Butler, R. N., 18, 74

Bynum, L. L., 33

Campbell, A., 35

Candy, P. C., 71

Capitol Community-Technical College (Hartford, Connecticut), 47

CD-ROM courses, 67, 68

Cerella, J., 29

Chambliss, L. N., 30, 31

Chautauqua movement, 5

Cherry, K. E., 32

Chiva, A., 18

City University Options for Older Learners (COOL), 47

Clough, B., 6

Cody, M. J., 65, 68

Cognition: age-related changes in, 28; as framework for older adult learning, 28–31; impact of noncognitive factors on, 28–29; and memory, 30–31; and older adult learning, 19; training interventions for improving, 29–30

Cohort-groups. *See* Generations

Cole, T. R., 18

Community of generations, 10

Computer technology: barriers to learning, 63–64; early adopters of, 62; future trends in, 67–71; model programs for, 64–67; profile of older users of, 61–62; training in, 46–47; usage statistics for, 61–62

Connecticut Institute for the Blind, 51

"Constructed Uses of Reminiscence Scale," 36

Contributive needs, 10

Cooper, K. L., 17

Coping needs, 10

Crook, T. H., 30

Cross, K. P., 42

Dekker, D., 18

Dellefield, K. S., 31

Deobil S., 20

Deptula, D., 31

Deutchman, D., 18

Dittmann-Kohli, F., 19

Dixon, R. A., 30, 31

Donahue, W. T., 6, 7, 56

Dubes, M. J., 34

Durr, D., 6

Earl, R., 51

Education for Later Maturity, 7

Educational gerontology: and adult education, 6–7; and aging of population, 1; and cognitive theory, 19; and computer

Tough, A., 58
Transcendence needs, 10
Troll, L. E., 17
Trott, J. W., 32
Turner, B. F., 17
Twitchell, S., 32

U.S. Department of Education, National Center for Education Statistics, 1
U.S. Department of Health and Human Services, 50
University of Kentucky Donovan Scholars Program, 6
University of Massachusetts–Boston, 57
University of North Carolina at Asheville (UNCA), 49
University of San Francisco, 65
University of Southern California, 65
Using Learning to Meet the Challenges of Older Adulthood, 85

Vaillant, C. O., 16, 18
Vaillant, G. E., 16, 18, 20
Valdiserri, M., 28, 30
Van Tassel, D. D., 18

Walker, J., 18
Walsh, D. A., 28
Waskel, S. A., 6
Webster, J. D., 18
WebTV, 68–69
Wendt, P. F., 33, 65, 68
Wenzel-Miller, L. A., 6
Werby, E., 20
Willis, S. L., 16, 18, 19, 29, 30
Wolf, M. A., 18, 19, 20, 41, 85
Wolfe, N. S., 34
World Wide Web (WWW), 68–69
Wright, J., 6

Youngjohn, J. R., 30

ORDERING INFORMATION

NEW DIRECTIONS FOR ADULT AND CONTINUING EDUCATION is a series of paperback books that explores issues of common interest to instructors, administrators, counselors, and policy makers in a broad range of adult and continuing education settings—such as colleges and universities, extension programs, businesses, the military, prisons, libraries, and museums. Books in the series are published quarterly in Spring, Summer, Fall, and Winter and are available for purchase by subscription and individually.

SUBSCRIPTIONS cost $54.00 for individuals (a savings of 35 percent over single-copy prices) and $90.00 for institutions, agencies, and libraries. Standing orders are accepted. New York residents, add local sales tax for subscriptions. (For subscriptions outside the United States, add $7.00 for shipping via surface mail or $25.00 for air mail. Orders must be prepaid in U.S. dollars by check drawn on a U.S. bank or charged to VISA, MasterCard, or American Express.)

SINGLE COPIES cost $22.00 plus shipping (see below) when payment accompanies order. California, New Jersey, New York, and Washington, D.C., residents, please include appropriate sales tax. Canadian residents, add GST and any local taxes. Billed orders will be charged shipping and handling. No billed shipments to post office boxes. (Orders from outside the United States must be prepaid in U.S. dollars by check drawn on a U.S. bank or charged to VISA, MasterCard, or American Express.)

SHIPPING (SINGLE COPIES ONLY): $30.00 and under, add $5.50; to $50.00, add $6.50; to $75.00, add $7.50; to $100.00, add $9.00; to $150.00, add $10.00.

ALL PRICES are subject to change.

DISCOUNTS FOR QUANTITY ORDERS are available. Please write to the address below for information.

ALL ORDERS must include either the name of an individual or an official purchase order number. Please submit your order as follows:
    Subscriptions: specify series and year subscription is to begin
    Single copies: include individual title code (such as ACE 59)

MAIL ALL ORDERS TO:
    Jossey-Bass Publishers
    350 Sansome Street
    San Francisco, CA 94104-1342

Phone subscriptions or single-copy orders toll-free at (888) 378-2537 or at (415)433-1767 (toll call).
Fax orders toll-free to (800) 605-2665

FOR SUBSCRIPTION SALES OUTSIDE OF THE UNITED STATES, contact any international subscription agency or Jossey-Bass directly.